Express
Winemaking

by

Ren Bellis

Printed in Great Britain by
St. Stephens Bristol Press Ltd.

1st Edition
1st Impression September 1979

SBN 0 900841 57 5

Cover by: Cassedy Russell Design.

Express
Winemaking

Contents

Index to Illustrations and Tables

Index to Express Recipes

CHAPTER ONE

Here's How

This is a volume dedicated to that large and rapidly growing section of our community who, in a world of Instant Everything, feel that that approach could well be applied to the production of wine. It is a *how* book rather than a *why* book; its sole purpose the putting of its reader in good spirits and good spirits into him, with nothing to prove but proof itself! And since the initial *how* of most newcomers to winemaking is "How soon can I drink it?" the justification for its title becomes immediately obvious.

It cannot be disputed that the great majority of wines improve immeasurably if left in bulk, and preferably in cask, to reach respectable maturity, but many really acceptable wines *can* be shuffled together in short time — to meet a sudden challenge or as a matter of economic expediency.

Making a start . . .

There is more than one way of making express wines. The first is easy, by using one of the several kits available. These divide into two groups, of identical purpose but dissimilar content. On the one hand we have truly complete packs mostly of Danish origin, which feature carefully balanced concentrations of apple, elderberry, redcurrant, rhubarb and other juices naturally rich in malic acid (see Table A).

All the fussing and figuring is done for us and supplementary ingredients are supplied, precisely weighed and individually packaged, for introduction on a "winemaking by numbers" basis.

Those with throats athirst, ignorant of even the most elementary winemaking procedures but curious, adventurous and anxious to head for gracious living in a determined sort of way, should have no difficulty at all in following the smoothed path such kits (covering a choice of red, white or rosé wines, several

TABLE A
The principal acids naturally present in some basic winemaking ingredients

Ingredient	Principal Acids	Content	Ingredient	Principal Acids	Content
Apples	M	High/med	Lemons	C	High
Apricots	M	Medium	Limes	C	High
Bananas	C	Low	Loganberries	C	High
Bilberries	M–C	Medium	Oranges	C–As.	High
Blackberries	M–C	High	Peaches	C	Medium
Blackcurrants	M–C	High	Pears	C	Low
Bullace	M	High	Plums	M	High
Cherries	M	Med/Low	Raisins	T	Medium
Cranberries	M–T–Bz.	Medium	Raspberries	C–I–M	High
Damsons	M	High	Redcurrants	C–M	High
Dates	—	Low	Rhubarb	M–Ox.	High
Elderberries	M–C	Low	Rosehips	M–As.	Low
Figs	—	Low	Rowanberries	M	Medium
Flower Petals	—	Low	Sloes	M	High
Gooseberries	C–M	High	Strawberries	M–C–Bz.	Medium
Grains	—	Low	Sultanas	T	Medium
Grapes	T-M	Medium	Tangerines	C	High
Grapefruits	C	High	Vegetables	—	Low
Greengage	M	High	Whitecurrants	C	High
Leaves	—	Low			

Note: This table presumes optimum ripeness in all cases.

KEY: M = Malic; C = Citric; T = Tartaric; As. = Ascorbic; Bz. = Benzoic; Ox. = Oxalic.

dessert wines and a number of vermouths) have to offer. They need only approach their local supply stores, speak up, and specify. They will, however, have to let go their hold on one particular prejudice that has, over many years, grown from a cobweb to a cable: the idea that good wine can only be made from grapes.

It is a complete fallacy that true and wholesome wine can only be made from grapes and concentrated grape juices. The literature of winemaking is top-heavy with recipes that prove otherwise, and most good wine merchants are able to offer grape-free vintages, underlining the point that such things not only *are* but have been right along. Nevertheless, for those who insist on using only grape juice, there are the increasingly popular grape-concentrate-and-packeted-yeast combinations. These are supplemented with glucose syrup in some cases and claim to require only the addition of water, relying for their efficiency upon a modest sugar content (capable of conversion to a frankly less-than-adequate alcohol strength) and an exceptionally high fermentation temperature in the region of 86°Fa. (30° Cent.). In this regard they are open to attack by their critics. Since, however, it is the purpose of this volume to guide rather than indulge in controversy, we will stick our necks out only to the point of saying that the two best-known require to be given the additional support of various aids and services common to good winemaking practice. They are, to that limited extent, incomplete.

Those who are prepared to be a little more adventurous may take the slightly stonier path of personal formulation and, at the end of it, reap the satisfaction of knowing themselves to be winemakers rather than just another someone who makes wine: a subtle distinction. They, too, have a choice of approach: they can purchase a commercially available "three-week power-pack" comprising all the supplementary ingredients (true wine yeast, pectin-destroying enzyme, Wyoming Bentonite, nutrient salts, fruit acids, grape tannin, stabilising compound, Campden tablets and a fining agent) common to the Danish kits, or they can try their hand by obtaining its several constituents, plus a few more inspirational and beneficent substances, as separate items, using them for any country wine according to the recommendations the following chapters have to offer.

CHAPTER TWO

Temperature: the controlling factor

According to war-time gossip issuing from the Pacific islands and other far-flung places, the green or "drinking" coconut has much to recommend it if only speed is the main consideration in domestic booze production.

The procedure was as follows:

An eye of the coconut was pierced to allow a couple of spoonfuls of sugar to be inserted. Then the eye was stoppered and Nature, in the tropics, did the rest in about four days. When the plug blew out, there was your toddy: capable of producing all the effects of a do-it-yourself tonsillectomy and ready in its own individual cup.

Since it is presumed that you are civilised in the matter of drinking, not just one of those oafs who drink solely to get drunk, such exercises are not for us. I mention the matter merely to make the point about the relationship of temperature to the speed of fermentation. Within a certain range, a rise in temperature means a faster fermentation.

	TEMPERATURE BELOW 55° Fa.	Most wine yeasts will lie dormant. Low temperatures never KILLED a yeast.
	TEMPERATURE 55°- 65° Fa.	The yeast will be contented but lazy, pressing on with the job of making alcohol without show or fuss.
	TEMPERATURE 66°-76° Fa.	The yeast at the top of its form and in a lively state.
	TEMPERATURE 77°-85°Fa.	Yeast raging, devastating any hope of bouquet and encouraging the development of off-flavours.
	TEMPERATURE 86° Fa. →	The yeast itself devastated.

TEMPERATURE AND YEAST REACTION   *Table B*

Assuming the absence of all disruptive circumstances, and with due emphasis placed on the fact that all figures quoted must be accepted as averages rather than certainties, the following temperature/time related schedule would apply to one or more gallons of potential wine intended to be of 10·6% alcohol strength (i.e. a red or white burgundy type initially containing 33 oz of sugar per gallon or, in metric terms, 206 gm per litre).

TABLE C

TEMPERATURE OF MUST		DURATION OF FERMENT
°Fa.	°Cent.	DAYS
77	25	21
75	24	22
73	23	23
71	22	25
70	21	28
68	20	32

Heavy dessert-type wines and vermouths, based on appreciably more sugar, will of course take longer to complete (five or more weeks in most cases) as will all wines put together during the winter months unless the temperatures quoted can be steadily maintained.

To this end there are a number of excellent gadgets on the market: electrically-heated belts, hot-plates and thermostatically-controlled immersion heaters of the 'tropical fish tank" type illustrated in Fig. 1. Of all such devices, however, the latter are a personal choice since these are designed to be fully submersible and thus control the temperature of the developing wine itself rather than that of the atmosphere around it. They are, nevertheless, frequently pre-set to provide 70°Fa (21° Cent) and then need to be re-adjusted (quite simply, by means of a small screw incorporated for the purpose) if the higher temperatures are one's aim. In this regard, 75°Fa (24° Cent) is a recommended setting, encouraging near-maximum yeast efficiency whilst making allowance for up to two degrees of extra heat which the energetic yeast cells may themselves produce: a circumstance that needs to be guarded against if a jar of wine, left to its own devices, is not to creep well beyond an acceptable temperature under the impulse of its own action, the yeast in consequence being devastated before fermentation is complete.

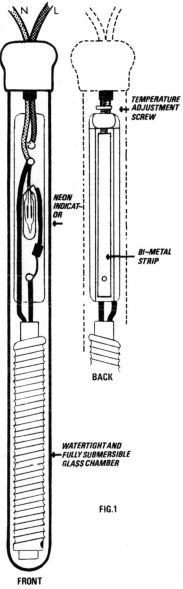

N L

TEMPERATURE
ADJUSTMENT
SCREW

NEON
INDICAT-
OR

BI-METAL
STRIP

BACK

WATERTIGHT AND
FULLY SUBMERSIBLE
GLASS CHAMBER

FIG.1

FRONT

Fig. 1
The "Uno" thermostatically-controlled heater. By turning the temperature-adjustment screw clockwise or anti-clockwise one may increase or reduce the thermostat setting according to need, a one-eighth turn of the screw being approximately equivalent to 7°Fa (3·75°Cent).

If, on the other hand, you would really like to step out a bit, the construction of a Fermentation Cabinet should be high on your list of do-it-yourself projects.

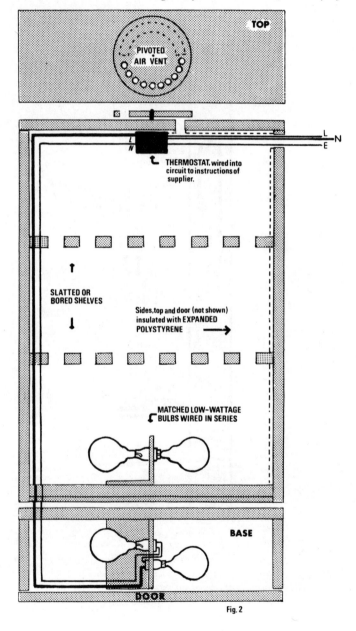

Fig. 2

An old, discarded, piece of junk furniture, brought from retirement or purchased for a song, can often be adapted to become the life and soul of the party. Alternatively, the unit can be constructed of 19 mm blockboard or plywood to exactly suit the dimensions of the fermentation vessels being used.

Essentially it consists of a cupboard with bored or slatted shelves (to permit the circulation of warm air) lined out with expanded polystyrene ceiling tiles and incorporating, in its base, two mounted electric light bulbs of low but identical wattage (Fig. 2).

In many cases bulbs of 15-watts or less will be found capable of maintaining the temperature required but final choice must, of course, be dictated by practical experiment having regard to cupboard size. Whatever the outcome of such tests, it is essential that the bulbs be wired "in series" as shown in the diagram. They will both, then, be working at only half their potential load, distributing their warmth evenly and having an almost indefinite life.

A 1-amp "air-type" thermostat — screwed below the top of the unit and connected to the mains supply in accordance with the instructions of its manufacturer — can subsequently be set to 75°Fa (24° Cent) and left to provide the restraint that is its justification. The top itself, gashed with a semi-circular 1-inch (25 mm) slot capped by a pivoted disc bored with a close series of 1-inch diameter holes, provides a means of manual temperature adjustment should this be called for.

In the absence of all such temperature-inducing devices as those referred to, at least be sure that your fermenting wine enjoys an *even* warmth, away from draughts and free of sudden temperature changes. To this end, and according to temperature conditions, wrap one, two or more sheets of flexible expanded polystyrene (the sort sold for application to walls prior to their being papered) around the fermenting vessels, holding them in place by means of rubber bands. The insulating "sleeves" thus formed, if of a height slightly in excess of the jars when fitted with an air-lock, will then allow for a square of polystyrene ceiling tile to be placed atop to form a lid.

CHAPTER THREE

Basic Equipment

Whatever your approach to winemaking, a number of utensils will obviously be required.

It has been said: if you had little more than a few empty bottles, a stretch of plastic and a rubber band you could still, theoretically and by applying a little ingenuity to the task of "making do", produce a sufficient quantity of good wine to fill them.

Only a masochist would embark twice on such a plan, and only a sadist (someone invariably kind to masochists) would suggest it. Nevertheless, one of the great features of home winemaking, express or not, is that expenditure can be regulated to suit one's inclination.

A good deal of the necessary equipment you doubtless have on hand right now. The rest can be divided into two categories: those items that are essential to even the simplest approach and those that can be done without but are nice to have around.

In the case of winemaking from kits and concentrates the bare minimum of equipment indispensable to good management will consist of:

(1) two suitable containers (one a spare for switching purposes) made of glass or plastic (I.C.I. "Alkathene", uncoloured polyethylene or polypropylene: materials approved for general use in connection with food products) of a capacity slightly greater than the volume of wine intended and capable of being fitted with an air-lock,
(2) a measuring jug,
(3) a large wooden or plastic spoon,
(4) a funnel,
(5) an air-lock fitted into a bored cork suited to the neck of the fermenting vessel, and
(6) a 5–6 ft (2 metres) length of rubber or plastic tubing attached to some form of sediment-trap device (see Fig. 9).

Because we are, on the whole, pretty poor guessers of sensible heat the purchase of a thermometer is, for most of us, a worthwhile investment: particularly if we intend to pursue our hobby more than just a little, making use of fresh fruits available for the picking and extracting their juices by enzymic means as described in Chapter 8. For the moment, however, we can "get by" if it is noted that one part of boiling water added to four parts of cold will register "lukewarm" (86°Fa or 30°Cent) whilst the same amount added to only two-and-a-half parts of cold will provide water at blood-heat (approximately 98°Fa or 37°Cent).

As regards item (1) of the list previously given, in some instances instructions accompanying the larger express kits advocate the use of $5\frac{1}{2}$-gallon (25 litre) carboys as fermentation vessels and subsequently suggest that these should, on specified occasions, be "shaken vigorously for about one minute": a recommendation (in the case of king-sized brews weighing upwards of half-a hundredweight) more easily voiced than achieved. If, therefore, you have reached an age when you feel disinclined to exercise anything but caution, have by you six inches or so of substantial dowelling (cut, perhaps, from the end of a broom handle) and place this centrally beneath any large container before it is filled. It will act as a pivot upon which the largest vessel and its contents may be energetically rocked without effort and serve to provide a tilt that assists closer racking when occasion demands.

There are, of course, new gimmicks and gadgets, in innumerable variations of style, quality, shape and transparency, coming out every day, but the two items most likely to come as strangers to the normal domestic scene are air-locks and sediment-traps. A few supplementary words concerning these helpmeets are, thus, appropriate.

Air-locks

These are simple but ingenious devices that work effectively to serve a double purpose.

Yeast demands oxygen for the carrying out of its reproductive process. Cut off from the generous supply air will provide, it is obliged to turn to some other source: the sugar with which we feed it. Working upon this for the satisfaction of its own needs, it reduces the ration (or, at least, as much as it can handle, for nature has decreed that all yeasts must work within well defined tolerances of alcohol strength) to produce almost equal parts of carbon dioxide gas and the alcohol we seek.

An air-lock serves, thus, as a spur to drive the yeast the way we want it to go and, at the same time, allows the unwanted gas (as much as one-hundred litres of it from each pound of sugar fermented to dryness) to escape into the atmosphere whilst preventing the ingress of any air.

Except in the case of "dry" locks (designed to operate on the rise and fall of a small bearing) all types are merely filled to a depth of half-an-inch or so with water (Fig. 3). From then on their action is automatic, a continuous procession of bubbles (running fast at first but slowing as fermentation nears its end) keeping the water pushed to one side (Fig. 4): an indication that the conversion of our sugar to alcohol is proceeding according to plan.

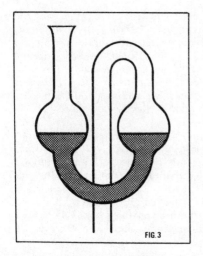

FIG. 3

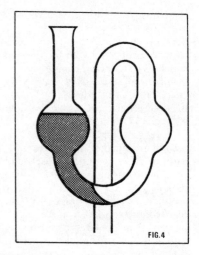

FIG. 4

The sight of a bubbling air-lock is, however, an open invitation to small fruit flies and similar insects. It is, therefore, wise to plug the open end of an uncapped lock with a small twist of cottonwool. Alternatively, use sulphite solution (see Chapter 4) in the lock instead of water. An additional drop of glycerine will avoid the possibility of an unattended lock drying out.

The "conventional" glass lock (item "A", Fig. 5) has long been the symbol of

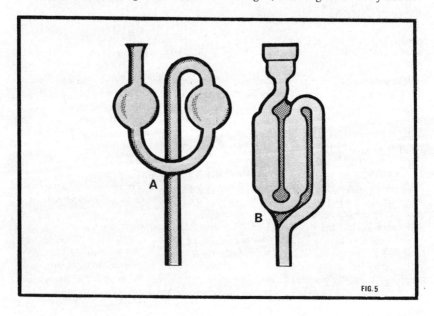

FIG. 5

amateur winemaking and its popularity has inevitably led to its near-reproduction in moulded plastic as shown at "B".

Several alternative designs, offering minor advantages, are nevertheless available.

One such, the glass "extended" lock, is illustrated in Fig. 6 comparing it, height for height, against the conventional pattern and underlining the benefit of its use on shelves where headroom is limited.

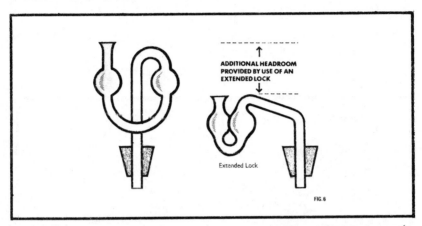

ADDITIONAL HEADROOM
PROVIDED BY USE OF AN
EXTENDED LOCK

Extended Lock

FIG. 6

Slightly different in concept but identical as regards performance are the several patent plastic locks available from most winemaking supply stores. Those shown here, from left to right of Fig. 7, are: (A) the "Handi" lock, inexpensive, complete with dust-cap and available in two sizes, (B) the "Vinty" pattern, fitted with a one-way pressure valve that enables it to be used with or without water content, and (C) the "Sentry" dry lock, entirely dependent on the function of a small one-way valve.

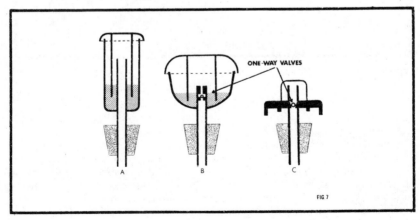

ONE-WAY VALVES

A   B   C

FIG 7

And here's a timely tip: a recommendation based on painful experience . . .

Glass air-locks, being in effect slender stems bent to a series of acute angles, are extremely fragile and require to be handled with the utmost care, particularly when being fitted with the bored cork or rubber bung essential to them.

To avoid unnecessary breakage at this time, with its attendant possibility of injury, ALWAYS twist the pre-softened cork (see page 68) ON to the lock: NEVER the lock INTO the cork (see Fig. 8).

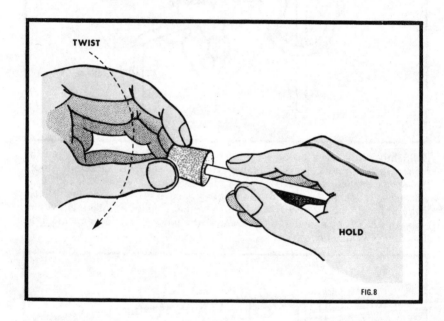

FIG.8

Sediment Traps

These may simply be a short length of glass tubing bent to a J-shape at one end or be of a more sophisticated type manufactured from either glass or plastic (Fig. 9). By their means the bulk of a wine may be siphoned ("racked") from vessel to vessel without any disturbance of the substantial deposit built up during the course of fermentation: a necessary procedure if off-flavours are to be avoided.

16

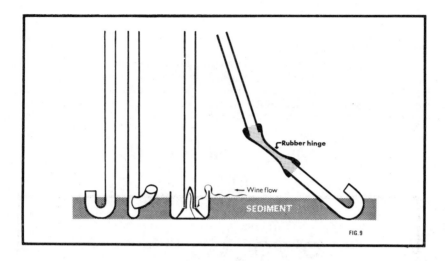

FIG. 9

In the case of the simple glass J-Tube, it is worth having this cut to two shorter lengths which may be hinged together by means of an inch or so of rubber tubing as illustrated. The trap end may then be so manoeuvred as to collect the maximum amount of sediment-free liquor without its container needing to be tilted.

Complete siphon units with in-built sediment traps are readily available in a variety of forms. Those shown here (from left to right of Fig. 10) are the "Vinty" adjustable siphon (with telescopic tube) and the "Colley" bulb-operated siphon-pump respectively.

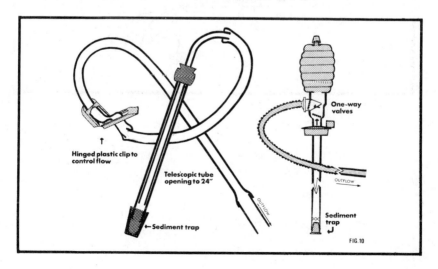

FIG. 10

Racking

The siphoning procedure itself is elementary but needs to be conducted with care.

Place the jar of wine to be transferred at a higher level than the empty vessel prepared to receive it (Fig. 11). Then, with the sediment-trap resting on the bottom of the filled container (its opening above the level of the deposit) suck on the free end of the tube until wine enters the mouth. A pinch applied to the tube will now hold the flow of wine until it can be directed into the waiting container.

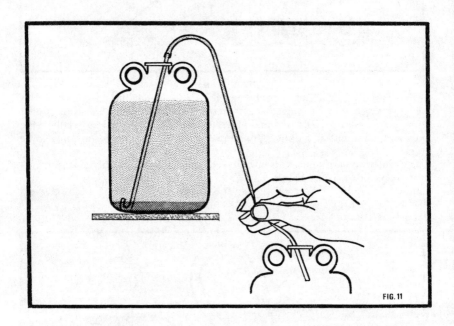

FIG. 11

CHAPTER FOUR

The Importance of "Absolute" Cleanliness

Whatever equipment you have elected to use, it will require a degree of treatment.

So far as the winemaker is concerned, there are two distinct states of cleanliness. The first is visual and said to be next to Godliness. The second borders on a condition of sterility and is next to impossible unless special care is taken to achieve it. No half measures will suffice, for sterility is like virginity: you either have it or you have not!

On our hands, on every item we intend to employ and everywhere about us are countless millions of rapidly multiplying wild yeast spores and acetic bacteria of all types. These are the enemies of good winemaking which, left unchallenged, will quickly convert our wine to vinegar, at which point other moulds and putrefactive agencies take over, breaking up the acetic acid (and almost everything else there is) and reducing all to its lowest possible stage: that is, to water, carbon dioxide gas and ammonium salts.

Fortunately, however, our defences against them are effective and easily applied. In spite of their wild ways they are pretty sensitive things, easily clobbered by sulphur dioxide: a pungent and penetrating gas conveniently accessible to the amateur through the salts of either sodium or potassium metabisulphite, the basis of officially approved Campden Fruit Preserving Tablets.

For the general preparation of vessels and utensils, therefore:

1.   Start by making sure that these are squeaky-clean, swilling them with a solution of one part of domestic bleach (e.g. Brobat) in nine parts of water if they come to hand very dirty or in a neglected condition.

2.   Rinse them thoroughly in running water, particularly if bleach has been used, since the slightest trace of this, left around to contaminate a fermenting wine, will produce a tang and bouquet more reminiscent of

decay and gunsmoke than a tree-roofed boulevard in Paris.

3. Make up a sulphite solution by dissolving half a teaspoon (2·5 gm) of sodium metabisulphite (or four Campden tablets) and half that quantity of either citric or tartaric acid in 1-pint (568 cc) of hot water.

4. Pour the resultant mix from one vessel to the next and sponge it over any other items to be treated. The equipment, then, needs merely be left to drain before use.

CHAPTER FIVE

A Closer Look at Kits and their Contents

It is to Denmark, a country of five million inhabitants and a high percentage of heroic thirsts, that we must look for the inspiration that lies behind methods which today, enable us to achieve one or more gallons of good wine in less time than it takes, applying normal procedures, to attain the earliest stages of fermentation.

It may, and probably will, be argued that there is nothing new about "instant" wine. No one, certainly, would claim originality for the idea of blending fruits and berries to provide a fermentable medium of grapejuice character and efficiency. Nevertheless, due credit must be paid to Master Winemaker K. L. Larsen of Tommerup for it was he who, in 1969, applied the previous twenty-five years of his experience in the trade to the task of assembling a complete and balanced kit capable of arousing interest amongst the many thousands lacking the time or inclination to await the outcome of months spent fermenting and maturing but who, on the other hand, felt a vital and growing need for an acceptable social lubricant.

At his say-so, combinations of apple, elderberry, redcurrant and other juices indigenous to the home acres stepped right in to take charge and (if sales statistics are anything to go by) the job is still theirs and likely to remain so.

Of the six "express" packs currently topping the popularity charts in Denmark (under the brand names of Auerbach, Heigar, Heriff, Larsen, Vigneron and Vinamat) only five have so far reached the British market.

TABLE D

Brand Name	Pack Size to make	Style	Main Distributor
Auerbach	—	—	Not currently available in this country.
Heigar	1-gallon 5-gallon	Red White Rosé	Rogers (Mead) Ltd, Shirlett, Broseley, Staffs
Heriff	1-gallon 5½-gallon	Sherry Kirseberry* Vin Rouge Vin Blanc Vin Rosé	Vina Ltd., 49 Marsh Lane, Bootle, Merseyside, L20 4HY
Larsen	2-gallon 4½-gallon 5-gallon	Campari Vin Rouge Vin Blanc White Vermouth Brown Vermouth Vin Rouge Vin Blanc Vin Rosé Rhine type Port Sherry Cherry Wine Amaro** Quinquina***	Larsen Wines UMK. Ltd., 87 Bedfont Lane, Feltham, Middlesex.
Vigneron	1-gallon 5-gallon	Vin Rouge Vin Blanc Vin Rosé Port Vin Rouge Vin Blanc Vin Rosé Port Vermouth Bianco Vermouth Rosso	Best Brews Ltd., 20 Queen Street, Horsham, Sussex, RH13 5AF.
Vinamat	2-gallon 5-gallon	Cherry Wine Dessert Wine Vermouth Vin Rouge Vin Blanc Vin Rosé	Home Winemaking Supplies, 12 The Hornet, Chichester.

22

* "Kirseberry": a cherry dessert wine that has been described as a cross between a Port and a low-strength liqueur.
** "Amaro": much darker than Campari.
*** "Quinquina": a tangerine-sherry.

Slight differences do occur, between one kit and another, as regards the nature of some additives supplied. In one case, for example, the necessary sterilising influence of sulphite rests upon the use of potassium metabisulphite whilst in others either sodium metabisulphite or sodium pyrosulphite are employed, but by itemising their contents in an orderly fashion, we can appreciate how all more or less conform to a standard pattern, i.e.:

TABLE E

ITEM	BRAND NAME				
	Herlff	Larson	Vigneron	Vinamat	Heigar
Wyoming Bentonite	*	*	*	*	*
Nutrient Salts	*	*	—	*	*
Wine Yeast	*	*	*	*	*
Potassium Sorbate	*	*	*	*	*
Sulphite Compound	*	*	*	*	*
Anti-pectin Enzyme	*	*	*	—	*
Supplementary Fining Agent	*	*	—	*	*
Tartaric Acid	—	*	—	—	—
Citric Acid	*	—	—	W	—

As regards the additives themselves: do not let their precise chemical names mislead you into thinking them unnatural or in any way foreign to wholesome wine production. Most of them have long been in use and will be recognised by experienced craft-workers as old friend .
Wyoming Bentonite, for example. . .
This special clay formed by the decomposition of volcanic ash under water (the correct grade for us being mined in a small area around Fort Benton in the State of Wyoming, U.S.A. from which it takes its name) has long been recognised as almost identical in composition to the so-called "Spanish Clay" that has, for many years, been used at Jerez for the treatment of the most delicate sherry wines. It has, in consequence, become familiar to experienced winemakers as a first-class fining agent for introduction to clouded wines immediately following the cessation of their ferment. Recently, however, experiments conducted in France and elsewhere have proved it capable of actually *speeding* a ferment (by reducing the protein concentration of a potential wine mix) if added at the rate of a teaspoonful (5 gms) per gallon *prior to yeast addition!*
Even in the case of aids that may be regarded as comparatively new to the cause (potassium sorbate, for instance, has only been available to U.K. winemakers following our entry to the Common Market) one has the assurance

that these have been tested and approved by a whole passel of leading authorities and have, like the shuntings and side-trackings we may be obliged to engage in, played their part in the preparation of many of the commercial products that lie behind the most respected labels.

But let us be more specific:

WYOMING BENTONITE

A light, pale grey, powder that will initially be found an unwilling mixer, it is most conveniently introduced in the form of a suspension that can be made up, bottled and stored ready for use as required. 1 oz. (30 gm. approximately) whisked into a small amount of cooled boiled water subsequently made up to 1-pint (568 cc.) will achieve the required balance but stirring should be strenuous and unremitting. Alternatively the slop may, as soon as possible, be transferred to a flat-bottomed bottle of a capacity somewhat greater than the volume intended for it. This will allow the suspension to be shaken and impacted periodically, as inclination dictates, over a period of twenty-four hours or so by the end of which time it will be ready to use at the rate of $3\frac{1}{2}$ fluid ounces (43 cc.) per gallon. If, meanwhile, the preparation has taken on the appearance of a thin gel, a swirl or two will quickly revert it to the state of a free-flowing liquid.

NUTRIENT SALTS

These are to yeast what K-rations are to the soldier on active service: a readily accessible and conveniently packaged supply of get-up-and-go!

Insofar as yeast is a plant it needs nitrogen, potassium and phosphorus, plus the stimulus of vitamins within the B_1 complex, for the encouragement of cell growth and, in consequence, a more rapid ferment.

There are a number of chemical compounds that can be added to a Must (the name we should apply to any combination of basic ingredients from which a wine is made) for the injection of these necessary influences. A teaspoon (5 gm) of ammonium phosphate, half-a-teaspoon (2·5 gm) of potassium phosphate and one tablet of aneurine or thiamine (backed by a mere pinch of magnesium sulphate — "Epsom Salts" — if the water supply is naturally soft) slipped into each gallon at the same time as the yeast will do an effective job.

The out-and-out newcomer to winemaking may, however, find it initially less troublesome to employ one of the several meticulously balanced proprietary compounds available from his local supplier. Of these, one of the best known is Tronozymol: a sophisticated single-shot additive composed of no less than nine action-getting substances (di-ammonium phosphate, ammonium sulphate, calcium phosphate, albumin, magnesium sulphate, disodium phosphate, potassium chloride, nicotinamide and aneurine hydrochloride).

Used at the rate of one teaspoonful (5 gm) per gallon (a standard dosage that may, quite safely, be exceeded should conditions call for such extravagance) this pharmacopoeia of nutrients and enzymes will quickly induce the maximum conversion of sugar to alcohol.

WINE YEASTS

Available under many brand names and representative of every well-known

24

wine type, true wine yeasts carry in their chromosomes certain characteristics of the soil from which they sprang, the climate in which they thrived and the vines upon which they developed. Their use, therefore, guarantees a pure and rapid fermentation of truly individual quality that the experienced craft worker can use to his considerable advantage (see Chapter 9).

The newcomer to winemaking is, however, advised to conduct his initial experiments with a good "general purpose" yeast, available from any wine-maker's supply store for only a few pence. This may be used satisfactorily in both red and white wines intended to be of table wine strength (not exceeding 15·6% alcohol) and offers the special advantage of conforming to a process of preparation that reduces to only an hour or so the two or more days of frustration that would, otherwise, need to be spent awaiting the start of fermentation proper.

Since it is difficult to be authoritative without expressing personal preferences it must be said that all yeasts packaged under the "Dane" brand label (produced by Danish Federation Industries Ltd. and distributed throughout the U.K. by Rogers (Mead) Ltd. Shirlett, Broseley, Staffordshire, conform excellently to the "express" method of activation detailed below, but many other well-known products (i.e. "Formula 67" and "Vinkwik") react just as admirably; nor must it be assumed that other brands are incapable of responding in a similar manner.

Method

Immediately prior to the carrying out of all other tasks associated with the formulation of a Must, take a cupful (4 fl. oz or 113 cc) of water at blood heat (98° Fa. or 37° Cent.) and to it add the general-purpose yeast in the quantity recommended by its manufacturer. Stir assiduously until a slight but permanent ring of minor bubbles becomes evident, then set the suspension to one side (not omitting to give it a further revivifying stir from time to time) for introduction as the final additive.

POTASSIUM SORBATE

Robert Burns it was who said: "The best-laid schemes o' mice an' men gang aft agley, an' lea's us nought but grief and pain for promised joy'."

Certain it is that nothing gangs quite so agley as a cherished but unstable bottle, proudly displayed, that suddenly shoots its cork through a puff of smoke and foams over the mahogany to finish up in your sock. For the prevention of such an occurrence various "stabilising" additives are widely employed but amongst all these potassium sorbate (a non-toxic compound long used in Europe, Canada and America) stands out like a peacock at a gathering of crows!

A most valuable aid to the halting of a ferment in the case of wines intended to remain sweet or medium-sweet, and a worthwhile precautionary addition to even those that are dry and thought to be inherently stable, it is available (sometimes under the title of Sorbistat K) from most good winemaker's supply stores.

A dosage rate of 1 gm. per gallon, first dissolved in 2 fl. oz (56 cc) of warm water, is appropriate but may present a problem to those not having facilities for the close measurement of such a quantity. It is, therefore, expedient to make up a stock solution by dissolving 1 oz (28 gm approximately) in warm water made up to 15 fl. oz (427 cc) when one tablespoon (15 cc) of the resulting solution will be equivalent to one gramme of the solid product. The dose should, however, be supplemented with at least one, but not more than two, Campden tablets per gallon if a slightly "geranium" bouquet is to be avoided.

SULPHITE COMPOUNDS
A correlationship exists between all forms insofar as one teaspoon (5 cc) of a Sodium Metabisulphite Stock Solution (prepared by dissolving 2 oz (56 gm) of sodium metabisulphite in a little water subsequently made up to 1-pint or 568 cc) equals one Campden tablet, in effect. It is, however, worth noting that the tablet's potassium content is useful as a yeast nutrient and can contribute to the reduction of a wine's excess acidity by encouraging this to crystallise out as tartar (potassium hydrogen tartrate, to give it a long name) and assisting the natural development of glycerine.

ANTI-PECTIN ENZYMES
Available under such brand names as Pectinol, Pektolase and Filtragol, these have as their purpose the degrading of pectin: a substance contained in some vegetables and all fruits in amounts varying according to the nature of the fruit itself. Bananas, for instance, have little of it. Strawberries, on the other hand, contain slightly more; apples, apricots and plums of every variety possess it in considerable quantity.

Capable of producing a state of gel in the presence of sugar and acid, pectin is the agent responsible for the setting of jams and jellies. Allowed to intrude upon a wine, however, it will inevitably cause the development of hazes that are difficult to clear. A teaspoon of any anti-pectin, added to each gallon of Must twenty-four hours or so before Bentonite addition, is thus a generous but worthwhile measure for the avoidance of subsequent trouble. A further benefit stems from the fact that, under its influence, lightly pulped fruit will yield a juice (flowing at least twenty-five per cent more generously than one obtained under any other form of treatment) of better colour, clarity and flavour than that obtained by heat application or mechanical means.

Even in the case of wines made from commercially available juices and concentrates the addition of an anti-pectin, in the quantity mentioned, is economically advantageous since these will then settle to clarity more quickly and provide a firmer sediment from which the finished product may be more closely racked.

SUPPLEMENTARY FINING AGENTS
It is in respect of these that the kit manufacturers are most at variance. Some consider them essential; some take the opposite view. In one case ("Larsen") a solution of zinc sulphate, gypsum and potassium aluminium sulphate is supplied for use in conjunction with yellow prussiate of potash. In another ("Vinamat") a solution containing thirty per cent of colloidally dispersed silicic acid is provided to work in partnership with gelatine. There are, nevertheless, a great number of organic, mineral and vegetable substances that can be used to induce the rapid

clearance of a young wine, and a wide range of proprietary products which, used in accordance with the instructions accompanying them, are capable of effecting the service. It makes good sense to have one of them by you. Regard it, however, as a last resource for use in emergency rather than as an item due for routine admission.

TARTARIC ACID

Because of its tendency to precipitate as soon as fermentation starts to produce alcohol in quantity (a process of retirement that can be speeded by holding the wine at a low temperature) this is a most accommodating additive with which to supplement the natural malic and/or citric content of fresh juices or concentrates not already balanced for acid by their manufacturers.

CITRIC ACID

Commonly employed for the balancing of wine Musts and commercial concentrates, this is the best known (and consequently the most misused) of all the natural fruit acids: a situation explained by the fact that citrus fruits were, for a long time, the only source of acid familiar to the country winemaker.

Capable of effecting a moderately fast ferment and responsive to a degree of control (insofar as any slight excess can either be precipitated by means of chalk or masked — a defeatist remedy — by a small addition of pure glycerine to the finished brew) its solo use in wine does, however, have one major disadvantage. It promotes a harshness of taste that takes a long time to mature out. The wise express operator reserves it, thus, for circumspect addition (in conjunction with tartaric and/or malic) to Musts of "medium" acidity based on ingredients such as apricots, cranberries, grapes, raisins and rowanberries from which it is notably absent (see Table A).

CHAPTER SIX

The First Gallons

In the sense that certain varieties require merely to be pressed and their juice left to ferment without need of further addition, apples are the only fruit indigenous to the Scandinavian countries and the United Kingdom from which anything like a true wine can be made.

The result of the most elementary treatment we know, of course, as cider. Used discriminately and given support, however, apples are capable of playing an effective part in the production of a wide range of quickly drinkable liquors indistinguishable from those of the grape. They contain a fairly high concentration of acid (principally malic) and tannin (essential to any wine if it is not to taste the way your foot feels when its asleep) under the combined influence of which fermentations are fast and trouble-free under all normal conditions and finished wines fall bright and clear without resort to a deal of fussing and finicking. Their sugar content, averaging about ten per cent of their picked weight, contributes a valuable 12 oz (340 gm) or so to each gallon of juice pressed from them and their flavour combines happily with that of the majority of other fruits and berries with which they may be partnered.

Unfortunately, apples at normal shop prices make nonsense of do-it-yourself economy, whilst those who are so fortunate as to have access to cheaper supplies are faced with the labour of pulping and pressing. The purchase of special gear with which to lighten these tasks is certainly not justified unless a considerable throughput is envisaged and even then, having regard to the seasonal nature of the work, much of the equipment is obliged to stand idle for the bulk of each year. Our initial interest should, thus, be directed towards the nine-times concentrated apple-juice with which every one of the Danish three-week wine kits is so generously boosted and bolstered. This is produced under vacuum conditions that prevent any deterioration of its qualities, and is available under labels such as those of Vina Home Winemaking Supplies (49 Marsh Lane,

Bootle), Ritchie Products (Rolleston Road, Burton-on-Trent) and the Country Wine Club (Drum Cottage, East Stourmouth, near Canterbury). Concentrated apple juice serves to reduce, in wines prepared from a mixed base, the time required for "open" ferments (thus diminishing the risk of bacterial contamination during this period when the Must is most vulnerable to attack) and enables five-gallon batches to be easily produced in a minimum of time and at a minimum of expense. Its mineral and tannin content suits it admirably for addition to honey-based formulations of the cyser (apple mead) type since honey is notably deficient in these essentials, and its inclusion in any standard honey-based recipe (according to taste and with allowance made for its natural sugar content) assures a more speedy and satisfactory fermentation in all cases.

Fruits which contain an over-abundance of tannin (and elderberries are remarkable in this respect, having a two-hundred to six-hundred per cent excess) present a problem insofar as wines made from them, in the quantities usually recommended, frequently require a prolonged maturing period to take the curse off them. By using a minimum of fruit and backboning the adjusted formulation by means of the concentrate, however, the possibility of a "thin" wine is avoided and the maturing period considerably reduced.

Individual winemakers, if and when the moment arrives for them to experiment on their own account, will no doubt discover for themselves the balance of this and that best suited to their individual requirements. In the meanwhile, to get you started, here are three detailed, tried, tested and easily managed recipes (for white, red and rosé wines respectively) requiring no more equipment than that already mentioned and no more understanding than that so far gained. For the sake of simplicity the specific products of particular manufacturers have been named. As previous pages have, however, pointed out: there are frequently other equally acceptable additives that may be used. If, therefore, the reader feels disposed to employ Pectinol rather than Pektolase, to substitute his own compounded form of nutrient for Tronozymol, or replace the Campden tablets with an equivalent number of teaspoons of Sodium Metabisulphite Stock Solution, he need not hesitate to do so.

Each one of the prescriptions can be relied upon to provide a result in weeks rather than months and if, by some mischance, they are not exactly suited to your taste, fear not! There will, I assure you, be some more along in a minute.

VIN BLANC EXPRESS No. 1

This is an economical, light and dry table wine (that may, however, be sweetened to taste) of about ten-per-cent alcohol (the approximate strength of a good white burgundy) upon which to put theory to the test.

Ingredients for 1-gallon

13–15 fl oz (369–426 cc) concentrated apple juice,
23 oz (651 gm) granulated sugar,
1 teaspoon (5 gm) Tronozymol yeast nutrient,
7 fl oz (86 cc) Wyoming Bentonite suspension made up as directed (see page 26),
1 teaspoon (5 gm) Pektolase (or any other anti-pectin enzyme),
1 tablespoon (15 cc) potassium sorbate solution made up as directed (see page 26),
2 Campden tablets (or two teaspoons — 10 cc) of Sodium Metabisulphite Stock Solution made up as directed: see page 26,
All-purpose wine yeast.

Method

1. To a cupful (4 fl oz or 113 cc) of water at blood heat (98°Fa or 37°Cent) add the wine yeast, in the quantity recommended by its manufacturer, and stir thoroughly for a minute or so until it is completely dispersed and a few light bubbles are evident. Then put the mix to one side for later use.
2. Into a clean and sterilised 1-gallon jar pour the apple concentrate. Add 2-pints (1·136 litres) of lukewarm water (86°Fa or 30°Cent) and shake both together.
3. Dissolve the sugar in 3½-pints (2 litres) of lukewarm water and add the resulting syrup to the now diluted concentrate, giving the fermenting vessel a further shake to ensure the proper involvement of its contents.
4. Measure out 3½ fl oz (43 cc) of the prepared Wyoming Bentonite suspension and add it to the other ingredients which should, once more, be stirred or otherwise agitated together.
5. Add one teaspoonful (5 gm) of Pektolase and one teaspoonful of Tronozymol to ½-pint (284 cc) of lukewarm water and stir well before leaving the solution to stand for about half-an-hour prior to its admission to the jar which should, subsequently, again be shaken very thoroughly.
6. Finally, swirl in the cupful of activated yeast previously set to one side. Seal the fermenting vessel with an air-lock fitted into a previously softened bored cork (see page 68) and set it in some place where a temperature of about 75°Fa (24°Cent) can be steadily maintained.

Fermentation should be evident within a matter of hours and truly vigorous only a short while later. All the time this continues, the jar and its contents should be given an energetic shake twice daily. When, however, the air-lock remains inactive over a prolonged period it may be assumed that the conversion of sugar to alcohol is complete and confirmation of the fact may be obtained from a trial sip of the still cloudy liquor in which not the slightest trace of sweetness should be apparent.

A factual record, based on such a production run and listing degrees of so-called "specific gravity" lost throughout tests conducted at regular 24-hour intervals, reads as follows:

Day 1. Specific gravity at start: 1·080
Day 2. Specific gravity down to: 1·044
Day 3. Specific gravity down to: 1·020
Day 4. Specific gravity down to: 1·010
Day 5. Specific gravity down to: 1·000
Day 6. Specific gravity down to: ·992

At this point:

7. Add a further 3½ fl oz (43 cc) of Wyoming Bentonite suspension and shake it thoroughly into complete involvement.
8. Dissolve two crushed Campden tablets in 2 fl oz (56 cc) of lukewarm water, stir in one tablespoon (15 cc) of potassium sorbate solution, and swill into the young wine.

   Shake all together; then allow the wine to stand for a further two days (under its protective lock) during which a periodic and lively agitation will ensure the complete removal of any carbon dioxide gas that may remain trapped in the liquor.
9. The wine, removed to a cool place, should now be allowed three days free of disturbance. Only following this pause period is it ready for transfer, by means of a siphon tube fitted with a sediment trap, from off its deposit into a second and thoroughly clean container. If, by some mischance, the sediment is disturbed during an early stage of the siphoning procedure: remove the tube, seal both the original and replacement jars with corks, and leave the wine for one or two days to re-settle.
10. When all the wine has been satisfactorily transferred, make up its volume to exactly 1-gallon using water that has been boiled and allowed to cool. Shake it well to remove any last vestiges of carbon dioxide gas that may remain within it; then leave it for a further seven days with the neck of its container plugged merely with a twist of cottonwool.
11. Taste some of your wine now to see if it suits your palate. Should it be too dry, dissolve 2 oz (57 gm) of sugar in 1-pint (568 cc) taken from the bulk and subsequently returned to sweeten the whole. Sampled after two days, the wine may show the marked improvement for which you are looking. If, however, an even greater degree of sweetness is required, repeat the process using only 1 oz (28 gm approximately) of sugar and again leaving for two days before trying.

VIN ROUGE EXPRESS No. 1

This is the Gay Dog: as lusty as it looks but star-bright within weeks and extremely fast maturing for all that.

Ingredients for 1-gallon

       13–15 fl oz (369–426 cc) concentrated apple juice.
       4 oz (113 gm) dried elderberries,
       1½ lb (680 gm) granulated sugar,
       1 teaspoon (5 gm) Tronozymol yeast nutrient,
       7 fl oz (86 cc) Wyoming Bentonite suspension made up as directed (see page 24),
       1 teaspoon (5 gm) Pektolase (or any other anti-pectin enzyme),
       1 tablespoon (15 cc) potassium sorbate solution made up as directed (see page 26),
       2 Campden tablets (or two teaspoons — 10 cc — of Sodium Metabisulphite Stock Solution made up as directed: see page 26),
       All-purpose wine yeast.

Method

1. Having activated the yeast and put it aside as the previous recipe suggests (see Vin Blanc Express No. 1), place the dried elderberries in a saucepan, cover with 1-pint (568 cc) of water, bring to boiling and allow to simmer for exactly fifteen minutes before straining off the juice. About 12 fl oz (341 cc) of liquor will result if the pulp is lightly pressed to obtain the maximum benefit from it.

2. To the apple concentrate (previously placed in a clean and sterile 1-gallon jar) add ½-pint (284 cc) of lukewarm water plus the elderberry juice. Shake all together and from this point proceed exactly as for Vin Blanc Express No. 1, dissolving the sugar in 3½-pints of lukewarm water and so on.

Those with an eye for such details will notice that the volume of Must, as initially put together, totals a volume one pint or so less than the gallon finally intended. This is good practice since, during the first 24-hours or so of fermentation, activity within the jar is likely to be vigorous, causing a frothy cap of rust-coloured solids to be pushed higher and higher. Space, therefore, should always be left for the accommodation of this since nothing is less calculated to induce a calm and co-operative domestic environment than the overnight arrival of a sunset mud-pool on the carpet!

Those of a nervous disposition may, indeed, consider it worthwhile to place the jar in a shallow bowl or plastic pail until the initial fermentation stage is over.

VIN ROSÉ EXPRESS No. 1

Rosé wines (half-castes, being neither white nor red) are said to owe their popularity among the British to our natural love of compromise. Be that as it may, here is a formulation that will be found accommodating in the extreme.

Scaled for the production of a 2-gallon batch that most conveniently accepts the 15 fl oz (426 cc) cans of Irish Roseberry Purée manufactured by Graham's of 216 Shore Road, Belfast, Northern Ireland but available from most winemaking supply stores, the quantities given in the list of ingredients can, of course, be reduced by half if only a 1-gallon volume of wine is required.

Ingredients for 2-gallons
>13-15 fl oz (369-426 cc) concentrated apple juice,
>15 fl oz (426 cc) Irish Roseberry Purée,
>1 lb (453 gm) bananas,
>4 fl oz (114 cc) strong cold tea,
>3 lb (1·360 kg) granulated sugar,
>2 teaspoons (10 gm) Tronozymol yeast nutrient,
>14 fl oz (⬛⬛⬛) Wyoming Bentonite suspension made up as directed (see page 24),
>2 teaspoons (10 gm) Pektolase (or any other anti-pectin enzyme),
>2 tablespoons (30 cc) potassium sorbate solution made up as directed (see page 26),
>4 Campden tablets (or four teaspoons — 20 cc — of Sodium Metabisulphite Stock Solution made up as directed: see page 26),
>All-purpose wine yeast.

Method
1. Peel the bananas (discarding the skins) and crush the fruit prior to boiling it in 2-pints (1·136 litres) of water for twenty minutes. Transfer the slop to an open pail and allow it to cool before adding the anti-pectin enzyme and covering it with a clean towel prior to leaving it overnight in a warm atmosphere (ideally about 70°Fa or 21°Cent).
2. Without applying undue pressure, strain off the juice and transfer it to a 2-gallon fermentation vessel.
3. Activate the yeast by stirring it briskly into 4 fl oz (114 cc) of water at blood heat and put it to one side for later use.
4. Add the apple concentrate, roseberry purée, strong cold tea and 6-pints (3·409 litres) of lukewarm water to the banana extract and swill all together.
5. Dissolve the sugar in 4-pints (2·272 litres) of lukewarm water and involve thoroughly with the other ingredients.
6. Measure off 7 fl oz (86 cc) of the Wyoming Bentonite suspension and add this to the jar which should, once more, be given an energetic shake to incorporate its contents.
7. Add the yeast nutrient and, finally, the yeast suspension previously put to one side.
8. Apply air-lock, place the fermentation vessel in a warm atmosphere (75°Fa or 24°Cent) and leave the Must to ferment to dryness. When this is achieved (with no trace of sweetness evident) add a further 7 fl oz of Wyoming Bentonite suspension and swirl it into complete involvement.
9. Dissolve four crushed Campden tablets in 4 fl oz (112 cc) of lukewarm water, stir in two tablespoons (30 cc) of potassium sorbate solution, and add to the young wine.

Shake all together; then allow the wine to stand for a further two days (under its protective lock) during which period an occasional lively agitation will ensure the removal of any carbon dioxide gas that may remain trapped within it.

10. The wine, removed to a cool place, should now be allowed three days free of disturbance. Only following this pause period is it ready for transfer, by means of a siphon tube fitted with a sediment trap, from off its deposit into a second and thoroughly clean container. If, however, it remains faintly hazy at the end of this time, clarify it with a reliable proprietary fining agent.

11. When all the wine has been satisfactorily transferred, make up its volume to exactly 2-gallons using water that has been boiled and allowed to cool.

    Shake it well to remove any last vestiges of carbon dioxide gas that may remain within it; then leave it for a further seven days with the neck of its container plugged with cottonwool.

12. Taste some of your wine now. Should it be too dry, dissolve 4 oz (114 gm) of sugar in 2-pints (1·136 litres) taken from the bulk and use this to sweeten the whole. Sampled after two days, the wine may show the marked improvement for which you are looking. If, however, an even greater degree of sweetness is required, repeat the procedure (using only 2 oz — 57 gm — of sugar) and again leaving for two days before trying.

CHAPTER SEVEN

Extending The Range

The recipes so far detailed had, as their sole purpose, the guidance and encouragement of the reader.

Now, however, we have time to be more expansive . . .

There are quick-frozen, canned or bottled juices, syrups, concentrates and compounds enough to keep the express winemaker forever exploring the counters and displays of his local store. Some are more suited to the production of medium-sweet wines than those of table type. Let us sort these out as we go, meanwhile offering a selection of Vin Extraordinaires for those anxious to get on with their express winemaking.

APPLE AND GRAPE
Making use of the bottled or canned apple and grape juices intended for table use and sold by most good grocers, this is a wine that has confused many an erudite and discriminating palate into thinking it a German hock or moselle, a sip of which can easily develop into a gulp. The somewhat difficult relationship of British to metric measures is responsible for the packing of the basic constituents in all manner of inconvenient quantities. To obtain the volume recommended by the following formulation, therefore, it may be necessary to purchase several small bottles with some left over which, no doubt, other members of the family will be glad to help disperse.

Ingredients for 1-gallon
        51 fl oz (1·5 litres) apple juice (NOT concentrate),
        25 fl oz (710 cc) white grape juice (NOT concentrate),
        28 oz (793 gm) granulated sugar,
        1 teaspoon (5 gm) tartaric acid,
        7 fl oz (86 cc) Wyoming Bentonite suspension,
        1 teaspoon (5 gm) anti-pectin enzyme,
        1 tablespoon (15 cc) potassium sorbate solution,
        2 Campden tablets,
        All-purpose wine yeast and nutrient salts.

Method

Having activated the yeast as previously described, place the sugar and tartaric acid in a saucepan, add 2-pints (1·036 litres) of water and bring to the boil, stirring occasionally with a wooden spoon until the crystals have completely dissolved.

Allow the syrup to simmer over a gentle heat for half-an-hour or so during which time it will develop a light straw (Booth's Gin) colour. At this point it should be removed from the stove, allowed to cool and, when only lukewarm, transferred to the fermentation vessel for combination with the apple and grape juices.

The addition of $3\frac{1}{2}$ fl oz (43 cc) of the prepared Wyoming Bentonite suspension, pectin-destroying enzyme and nutrient salts then follows in accordance with stages 4 and 5 of the original Vin Blanc Express No. 1 recipe which further details the procedure to be subsequently adopted.

APPLE AND BLACKCURRANT

Everybody knows that malt (available in either liquid or dried extract form) constitutes the basis of all good beers. It is not so well known that a small quantity, slipped into any wine formulation, can save both time and money. In the case of wines made from plums, raspberries or cherries (fruits notorious for the enormous amount required if the products made from them are not to "drink thin") it may be regarded as an economic necessity. Here, however, it is associated with the blackcurrant syrup, sold under the brand name of "Ribena", to be obtained from most chemists.

The dry cider is incorporated as an alternative to the use of apples in any other guise.

Ingredients for 1-gallon

12 fl oz (340 cc) "Ribena" blackcurrant syrup,
4-pints (2·273 litres) dry cider,
4 oz (113gm) dry malt extract,
2 lb (907 gm) granulated sugar,
1 teaspoon (5 gm) tartaric acid,
7 fl oz (86 cc) Wyoming Bentonite suspension,
1 teaspoon (5 gm) anti-pectin enzyme,
1 tablespoon (15 cc) potassium sorbate solution,
2 Campden tablets,
All-purpose wine yeast and nutrient salts.

Method

Having activated the yeast and put it to one side in the usual manner, stand the open bottle of blackcurrant juice in a saucepan of water and gradually raise the temperature to 177°Fa (80°Cent) for ten minutes in order to drive off any sulphite preservative that may have been used in its preparation. Then swill the juice, still hot, into the cider and transfer both to the fermenting vessel.

Add the dry malt extract (dissolved in ½-pint (284 cc) of lukewarm water) and shake all together.

Place the sugar and tartaric acid in a saucepan, pour on 1-pint (568 cc) of water and bring to the boil, stirring occasionally with a wooden spoon until the crystals have completely dissolved.

Allow the syrup to simmer over a gentle heat for half-an-hour or so during which time it will develop a light straw colour. At this point allow it to cool and, when only lukewarm, funnel it into the other ingredients, making sure that all are thoroughly involved. The addition of 3½ fl oz (43 cc) of Wyoming Bentonite suspension, pectin-destroying enzyme and nutrient salts then follows in accordance with the Apple and Grape formulation previously given.

ORANGE AND GRAPE

Generally speaking, canned orange juices — sometimes evidencing a trace of bitterness that is inclined to creep through — are best reserved for the production of medium-sweet "social" or sweet "dessert" wines, both of which are a good deal more flavoursome and pushful than anything likely to be drunk with a meal. The recipe that follows incorporates, therefore, the quick-frozen product packaged behind Birds Eye Florida and Findus Jaffa labels.

Ingredients for 1-gallon
>   12 fl oz (341 cc) frozen orange juice,
>   25 fl oz (710 cc) white grape juice (NOT concentrate),
>   28 oz (793 gm) granulated sugar,
>   1 teaspoon (5 gm) tartaric acid,
>   7 fl oz (86 cc) Wyoming Bentonite solution,
>   1 teaspoon (5 gm) anti-pectin enzyme,
>   1 tablespoon (15 cc) potassium sorbate solution,
>   2 Campden tablets,
>   All-purpose wine yeast and nutrient salts.

Method
Activate the yeast in the usual manner and, having put it to one side pending further developments, make up the orange juice to 2-pints (1·137 litres) using lukewarm water. Then dissolve the sugar and acid in 3½-pints (2 litres) of lukewarm water and combine the resultant thin syrup with both the orange dilution and grape juice in the fermenting vessel.

Stir the anti-pectin and nutrient salts of your choice into ½-pint (284 cc) of water and (except for an occasional rouse) leave for half-an-hour or so before adding, together with 3½ fl oz (43 cc) of Wyoming Bentonite suspension, to the other ingredients.

Swirl everything together, ensuring their proper involvement, prior to adding

37

the activated yeast and applying an air-lock; then, when the young wine is down to complete dryness, proceed as from Stage 7 of the original Vin Blanc Express No. 1 recipe.

ROSEHIP
Notable for their high Vitamin C (ascorbic acid) content, rosehips are available to the all-year-round winemaker in many forms: as dried fruits, crisp shells, purées and syrups. It is with these latter, nestling on the chemist's shelves under names such as "Delrosa", "Hipsy" and "Optrose", that we are currently concerned for they make excellent express wines that are both quick to clear and fast to mature.

Ingredients for 1-gallon
    12 fl oz (341 cc) rosehip syrup,
    28 oz (793 gm) granulated sugar,
    $\frac{1}{2}$-teaspoon (2·5 gm) citric acid,
    $\frac{1}{2}$-teaspoon (2·5 gm) tartaric acid,
    7 fl oz (86 cc) Wyoming Bentonite suspension,
    1 teaspoon (5 gm) anti-pectin enzyme,
    1 tablespoon (15 cc) potassium sorbate solution,
    2 Campden tablets,
    All-purpose wine yeast and nutrient salts.

Method
Activate the yeast as in all previous cases and treat the bottle of syrup as for the blackcurrant, removing its cap, placing it in a saucepan of water and gradually raising its temperature to 177°Fa (80°Cent) for ten minutes prior to swilling its contents into 4-pints (2·273 litres) of cold water.

    Dissolve the sugar, together with the citric and tartaric acids, in 1$\frac{1}{2}$-pints (852 cc) of lukewarm water and shake both solutions together in the fermenting vessel.

    Add the anti-pectin and nutrient salts to $\frac{1}{2}$-pint (284 cc) lukewarm water, stir thoroughly and allow to stand for half-an-hour or so; then involve with the other ingredients before introducing 3$\frac{1}{2}$ fl oz (43 cc) of Wyoming Bentonite suspension, shaking all together and swirling in the now activated yeast previously put to one side. From this point, following the fermentation of the wine to dryness, proceed as from Stage 7 of the original Vin Blanc Express No. 1 recipe.

TEA AND APPLE
The formulation that follows is surprising: not only on account of its economy but because the final product — a dry white table wine — is more like a red wine in character.

    The "Earl Grey's" tea recommended is a large-leaf China blend which can be had from good grocers and most tea-merchants. It is not advisable to substitute Indian or Ceylon tea without a trial to determine the amount necessary, such teas being much stronger in colour, flavour and tannin content. Other grades of China tea can, however, be used.

Ingredients for 1-gallon

$\frac{1}{2}$-oz (15 gm approximately) Earl Grey's tea,
7$\frac{1}{2}$ fl oz (213 cc) apple concentrate,
28 oz (793 gm) granulated sugar,
$\frac{1}{2}$-teaspoon (2·5 gm) citric acid,
7 fl oz (86 cc) Wyoming Bentonite suspension,
1 teaspoon (5 gm) anti-pectin enzyme,
1 tablespoon (15 cc) potassium sorbate solution,
2 Campden tablets,
All-purpose wine yeast and nutrient salts. (NOTE: unless a proprietary nutrient such as Tronozymol is used, the fermentation will benefit from the addition of a tablet of Aneurine or Thiamine — Vitamin B^1 — to the prepared Must).

Method

Having activated the yeast in the appropriate manner, put it to one side and infuse the tea by pouring on 4-pints (2·272 litres) of boiling water; then leave for ten minutes before straining the hot liquor on to the sugar (stirring well to ensure that this is dissolved) and leaving to cool.

Add the concentrate, acid, nutrient salts and vitamin tablet (if used) to 1$\frac{1}{2}$-pints (852 cc) of lukewarm water and stir well before combining both solutions, by means of vigorous shaking, in the fermentation vessel.

Rouse the anti-pectin enzyme into $\frac{1}{2}$-pint (284 cc) of lukewarm water and leave for half-an-hour or so before swirling into the other ingredients. Then add 3$\frac{1}{2}$ fl oz (43 cc) of Wyoming Bentonite suspension, shake all together, top the fermenting vessel with an air-lock and ferment the wine to dryness before proceeding as from Stage 7 of the original Vin Blanc Express No. 1 recipe.

CHAPTER EIGHT

Increasing the Quality but Cutting the Cost

Don Quixote it was who said: "I drink upon occasion and sometimes I drink upon no occasion!".

If, therefore, you just have the urge for a party, need to face an onslaught of family members, or are called upon to dispense refreshment to a passel of nymphs and satyrs who have mistaken your home for the country club, wines made from kits, concentrates and the sundry items so far discussed will see you through right handsomely. Amongst a crowd they go down just as easily as a good many commercial products, winking behind fancy labels, that any clown with the price can buy.

But consider: there will come moments that call for the creation of a lasting impression, when only the best is good enough, and — no matter how efficiently they are processed — packaged juices can never quite capture all the elusive flavours and aromas of the fresh product. Let us now, therefore, turn our attention to the fully ripened orchard and hedgerow fruits (often left to rot but available for the picking) that we might persuade into our fermentation jars for the benefit of all the good things they have to offer.

Our aid in the matter is a further enzyme, Rohament P, that falls into effective collaboration with any type or brand of anti-pectin with which it may be partnered. Capable of breaking down and dissolving the cellular tissues that provide our fruits with their familiar shape and form, it enables us, quite easily, to produce purées from which the juice, clarified by simultaneous pectinase activity, flows freely (without need of heat application or special equipment) whilst retaining all the natural sugars, colour and flavour of its source. Prolonged and messy "fermentations on the pulp" (often advocated but frequently responsible for the disappointment of those who find their cherished gallons emerge raw and reeking) are rendered unnecessary and the subsequent routines of express winemaking, as already established, become a natural progression.

Applied at a dosage rate of half-a-teaspoon (2·5 gm) per six pounds (2·722 kilogrammes) weight of lightly crushed material (and if your hand shakes over-generously whilst dispensing the ration it hardly matters for, in dealing with enzymes, generosity pays off to one's advantage) Rohament P immediately works to break down the mass, reducing this to a slop of individual cells within hours if left to work its magic in a warm atmosphere of 70°-80°Fa (21°-26°Cent).

It is best incorporated, together with a teaspoonful of some anti-pectin, when dissolved or suspended in a small amount of free juice or water prior to its addition to the main bulk of materials which should, at the same time, be sulphited (at the rate of one Campden tablet for every four to six pounds weight) in order to kill off the wild yeasts amongst them and for their protection against the possibility of bacterial contamination. An initial tendency for some fruits to be slightly bleached by the sulphite is no cause for concern since their full colour will return within a very short while.

Frequent stirring of the combined mass during its treatment is essential if substantial temperature differences within it, leading to uneven processing, are to be avoided. Extended processing, at temperatures slightly higher than those quoted for guidance purposes, may, however, be indulged in quite safely, merely having the effect of thinning the juice and making it more amenable to separation from desiccated waste matter when the soup of lavished material and moisture is hand-pressed through a previously scalded cloth.

The process takes almost as long in the telling as in its application. It is, therefore, worth anybody's while to put it to the test, using one or other of the following compounded elixirs as a guide. And since green gooseberries are the first fruits of the year to be ready for the pot, it is appropriate that we should use them (in conjunction with one or two other inspirational items) for the purpose of detailing a few initial for-instances.

GOOSEBERRY AND APPLE

Ingredients for 1-gallon
>   2lb (907 gm) ripe green gooseberries,
>   7½ fl oz (213 cc) apple concentrate,
>   27 oz (765 gm) granulated sugar,
>   ¼ teaspoon (2·5 gm) Rohament P,
>   1 teaspoon (5 gm) anti-pectin enzyme,
>   7 fl oz (86 cc) Wyoming Bentonite suspension,
>   1 tablespoon (15 cc) potassium sorbate solution,
>   3 Campden tablets,
>   All-purpose wine yeast and nutrient salts.

Method
Day 1: Wash, top, tail and halve the gooseberries, place them in a plastic pail or equally suitable open vessel and pour on 2-pints (1·136 litres) of boiling water. Leave till only lukewarm, then pulp the fruit between the fingers and add one Campden tablet, the anti-pectin enzyme and Rohament P: all three dissolved

together in a little of the free juice.

Stir well to ensure even processing before covering with a clean towel and leaving in a warm atmosphere (70°–80°Fa or 21°–26°Cent) for 24 hours or so.

Day 2: Activate the yeast in the usual manner and put it to one side. Transfer the slop of gooseberry pulp and liquor to a straining bag that has been wrung dry after being plunged in boiling water and apply hand pressure to obtain the maximum amount of juice from it.

Discard the pulp and combine the juice with the apple concentrate in a 1-gallon fermentation jar.

Dissolve the sugar and nutrient salts in 4-pints (2·273 litres) of lukewarm water and swill the resulting thin syrup into the other ingredients before adding 3½ fl oz (43 cc) of Wyoming Bentonite suspension and the activated yeast previously prepared.

Shake the fermentation jar vigorously to thoroughly incorporate its contents before applying an air-lock and proceeding (once the wine has achieved dryness) as from Stage 7 of the original Vin Blanc Express No. 1 recipe.

GOOSEBERRY AND BANANA

Ingredients for 1-gallon
>   3 lb (1·360 kilos) ripe green gooseberries,
>   3½ oz (99gm) dried bananas,
>   4 fl oz (113 cc) strong cold tea,
>   2 lb (907 gm) granulated sugar,
>   ½ teaspoon (2·5 gm) tartaric acid,
>   ½ teaspoon (2·5 gm) Rohament P,
>   1 teaspoon (5 gm) anti-pectin enzyme,
>   7 fl oz (86 cc) Wyoming Bentonite suspension,
>   1 tablespoon (15 cc) potassium sorbate solution,
>   3 Campden tablets,
>   All-purpose wine yeast and nutrient salts.

Method

Day 1: Wash, top, tail and halve the gooseberries before placing them in a plastic pail. Mince the dried bananas into a saucepan, cover them with 2-pints (1·137 litres) of water and boil to a thin purée; then empty the contents of the saucepan, still hot, on to the berries which, when cool, should be crushed by means of a wooden stave or potato masher.

Combine the Rohament P, anti-pectin and one powdered Campden tablet in 1-pint (568 cc) of lukewarm water and add the solution to the slop of fruit, stirring well to ensure even processing before covering the pail with a clean towel and leaving it in a warm atmosphere (70°–80°Fa or 21°–26°Cent) for 24-hours or so.

Day 2: Having activated the yeast in the usual manner, strain the mix of gooseberry and banana juice into the fermentation vessel as previously described. Dissolve the sugar, acid and nutrient salts in 3-pints (1·705 litres) of lukewarm water, add the strong cold tea, and swill the entire mix into the fruit juices before adding 3½ fl oz (43 cc) of Wyoming Bentonite suspension.

Shake the jar well to ensure the proper involvement of its contents, then pour in the prepared yeast and cap it with an air-lock.

When the wine is down to dryness, with no evidence of sweetness apparent to the palate, proceed as from Stage 7 of the original Vin Blanc Express No. 1 recipe.

GOOSEBERRY AND GRAPE

Ingredients for 1-gallon
> 2 lb (907 gm) ripe green gooseberries,
> A2½ can (1 kg) white grape concentrate,
> 8 oz (226 gm) granulated sugar,
> ½ teaspoon (2·5 gm) Rohament P,
> 1 teaspoon (5 gm) anti-pectin enzyme,
> 7 fl oz (86 cc) Wyoming Bentonite suspension,
> 1 tablespoon (15 cc) potassium sorbate solution,
> 3 Campden tablets,
> All-purpose wine yeast and nutrient salts.

Method
Day 1: Prepare the fruit exactly as for the "Gooseberry and Apple" recipe.
Day 2: Activate the yeast and, having put it to one side, transfer the strained gooseberry juice to a 1-gallon fermentation jar.

Dilute the white grape concentrate with 1½-pints (852 cc) of hot (not boiling) water and add, shaking the vessel energetically to ensure the incorporation of its contents.

Dissolve the sugar and nutrient salts in 2-pints (1·137 litres) of lukewarm water, combine the resulting thin syrup with the other ingredients and pour in 3½ fl oz (43 cc) of Wyoming Bentonite suspension. Swirl everything together, add the activated yeast and seal the jar with an air-lock before establishing it in the warm place allocated.

When the wine is down to dryness, treat it as from Stage 7 of the original Vin Blanc Express No. 1 recipe.

GOOSEBERRY AND SULTANA

Ingredients for 1-gallon
> 3 lb (1·360 kilos) ripe green gooseberries,
> 1lb (453 gm) sultanas,
> 24 oz (680 gm) granulated sugar,
> ½ teaspoon (2·5 gm) Rohament P,
> 1 teaspoon (5 gm) anti-pectin enzyme,
> 7 fl oz (86 cc) Wyoming Bentonite suspension,
> 1 tablespoon (15 cc) potassium sorbate solution,
> 3 Campden tablets,
> All-purpose wine yeast and nutrient salts.

Method

Day 1: Soak the sultanas in water for half-an-hour or so before washing them thoroughly in running water to remove any preservative matter or mineral oil (usually liquid paraffin) that may have been used to keep their skins glossy and attractive for display purposes. Then chop them with a sharp knife and to them add the washed, topped, tailed and halved gooseberries.

Pour 3-pints (1·704 litres) of boiling water on to the combined fruits and, when cool, pulp them between the fingers prior to adding one crushed Campden tablet, the anti-pectin enzyme and Rohament P. Stir all together, cover with a clean towel, and leave in a warm atmosphere for 24-hours or so before straining off the juice for transfer to the fermenting vessel.

Day 2: Activate the yeast by stirring it into a cupful of water at blood heat and set it to one side whilst dissolving the sugar and nutrient salts in 4-pints (2·273 litres) of lukewarm water.

Add the sugar and nutrient solution to the fermentation jar, shaking the latter well to incorporate its contents, and pour in 3½ fl oz (43 cc) of Wyoming Bentonite suspension.

Shake the jar yet again, seal it with an air-lock and, as soon as fermentation ceases, proceed as from Stage 7 of the original Vin Blanc Express No. 1 recipe.

Let us, now, turn our thoughts to red and rosé wines and the autumn fruits that so ably provide them. Elderberries, for instance. As in all cases, care begins with the selection of ingredients. There are many varieties of elder, some more suited to winemaking than others. Leave to the birds, therefore, any temptingly black and glossy fruits that reveal a trace of green pulp when pressed between the fingers and (since petrol and diesel fumes are very pervasive) do your harvesting from hedgerows that border quiet country lanes rather than main roads.

A "straight" elderberry wine, based on 3 lb of fruit to the gallon, can be very fine if given plenty of time in which to mature and lose its initial tannin roughness which, sampled too soon, can take you by the throat and pull your tongue to an elongated lover's-knot. Used circumspectly, however, and blended with raisins as in the following formulation, a very acceptable and quickly drinkable vin ordinaire results.

ELDERBERRY AND RAISIN

Ingredients for 1-gallon

1 lb (453 gm) strigged elderberries,
1 lb (453 gm) raisins,
3 fl oz (85 cc) apple concentrate,
24 oz (680 gm) granulated sugar,
1 teaspoon (5 gm) tartaric acid,
½ teaspoon (2·5 gm) Rohament P,
1 teaspoon (5 gm) anti-pectin enzyme,
7 fl oz (86 cc) Wyoming Bentonite suspension,

1 tablespoon (15 cc) potassium sorbate solution,
3 Campden tablets,
All-purpose wine yeast and nutrient salts.

Method

Day 1: Soak, wash and chop the raisins and combine them with the elderberries in a plastic pail or other suitable vessel. Crush all together and pour on 4-pints (2·273 litres) of water in which one Campden tablet, the anti-pectin and Rohament P have been dissolved.

Stir thoroughly before covering with a clean towel and placing in a warm atmosphere for 24-hours or so at the end of which time the juice will be ready for straining off, under light pressure, into a 1-gallon fermentation jar.

Day 2: Activate the yeast. Dissolve the sugar, tartaric acid, apple concentrate and nutrient salts in 2½-pints (1·420 litres) of lukewarm water and add to the fermenter, shaking this well to ensure the complete involvement of its contents.

Swirl in 3½ fl oz (43 cc) of the Wyoming Bentonite suspension and pour in the activated yeast previously put to one side.

Fit air-lock, ferment the wine to dryness and subsequently proceed as from Stage 7 of the original Vin Blanc Express No. 1 recipe.

RED AUTUMN

This is the one wine to which a special title is applied; one made necessary by the fact that its fresh fruit contents, named in full, would never fit comfortably across a label. Since all, however, can be harvested at the same time of year, no trouble should be experienced in getting them together.

Those folk living close to moors upon which the bilberries grow wild have an obvious economic advantage, but 4 oz (113 gm) of the dried product or 16 oz (453 gm) of frozen blueberries make conveniently accessible substitutes. As regards the wild blackberries: choose those found growing in the hedges rather than in woodland areas (which tend to ripen earlier but are of inferior flavour) and sort them carefully, discarding any that evidence a trace of green.

Ingredients for 1-gallon
>2 lb (907 gm) wild blackberries,
>1 lb (453 gm) fresh bilberries,
>1 lb (453 gm) elderberries,
>1 lb (453 gm) sultanas,
>24 oz (680 gm) granulated sugar,
>1 teaspoon (5 gm) tartaric acid,
>1 teaspoon (5 gm) anti-pectin enzyme,
>¼ teaspoon (2·5 gm) Rohament P,
>7 fl oz (86 cc) Wyoming Bentonite suspension,
>1 tablespoon (15 cc) potassium sorbate solution,
>3 Campden tablets,
>All-purpose wine yeast and nutrient salts.

Method

Day 1: Soak and wash the sultanas before rough chopping them into $3\frac{1}{2}$-pints (2 litres) of water in which one Campden tablet has been dissolved. Sort and wash the berries, place them in a bowl and lightly pulp them with a wooden spoon before tipping them into the lightly sulphited water.

Add the anti-pectin and Rohament P. Stir to ensure even processing, then cover with a clean towel before placing in a warm atmosphere for 24-hours or so.

At the end of this time, strain off the juice (lightly pressing any remaining solid matter to secure the maximum benefit from it) and funnel it into the fermenting vessel.

Day 2: Activate the yeast as for all previous recipes and set it to one side.

Dissolve the sugar, acid and nutrient salts in 3-pints (1·704 litres) of lukewarm water and add the resultant thin syrup to the strained juice, swirling it well into complete involvement.

Pour in $3\frac{1}{2}$ fl oz (43 cc) of Wyoming Bentonite suspension and, having shaken it into complete dispersion, top off with the activated yeast before applying an air-lock, fermenting the liquor to dryness and proceeding as from Stage 7 of the original Vin Blanc Express No. 1 recipe.

BLACKCURRANT AND SULTANA ROSÉ

"We must buy currants for our wine" wrote Jane Austen to her sister Cassandra in June 1811, for of all the homemade acquaintance-riggers offered at that time, currant wine was the most popular.

Considered by some contemporary palates to have too dominant a flavour when used on their own, the black variety — introduced in small amounts — certainly lend themselves admirably to the rapid production of fast fermenting wines of rosé character. It is, however, essential (for the avoidance of excess tannin) that a watchful eye be kept on the colour of the juice during the course of its extraction by Rohament P treatment which should, consequently, be brought to an end (in the manner soon described) as and when a satisfactory deep rose hue is obtained.

Ingredients for 1-gallon
> 12 oz (340 gm) blackcurrants,
> 16 oz (453 gm) sultanas,
> 24 oz (680 gm) granulated sugar,
> 1 teaspoon (5 gm) tartaric acid,
> 1 teaspoon (5 gm) anti-pectin enzyme,
> $\frac{1}{2}$ teaspoon (2·5 gm) Rohament P,
> 7 fl oz (86 cc) Wyoming Bentonite suspension,
> 1 tablespoon (15 cc) potassium sorbate solution,
> 3 Campden tablets,
> All-purpose wine yeast and nutrient salts (supplemented with 1 Vitamin B[1] tablet for best results).

Method

Day 1: Soak, wash and chop the sultanas. Sort the blackcurrants, removing any stalks before washing them, adding them to the other fruit and crushing all together in a plastic pail.

Pour on 4-pints (2·273) of water and stir in one Campden tablet, the anti-pectin enzyme and Rohament P

Cover the treated mix with a clean towel and place it in a warm atmosphere (70°-80°Fa or 21°-26°Cent) until it has assumed a depth of colour considered appropriate for the type of wine being made. Then transfer it to a large saucepan and heat it to within the range of 151°-162°Fa (66°-72°Cent). These temperatures, though high enough to inactivate the enzymes themselves, will not impair the colour, flavour or vitamin content of the juices subjected to their influence. Finally, strain off the free juice (as hot as possible) and transfer it to the fermentation vessel in which it should be allowed to cool.

Day 2: Proceed exactly as for the previous recipe "Autumn Red".

CHAPTER NINE

Increasing the Strength

This chapter calls for what might be described as a Bold Stand. All the wines so far discussed, adequate substitutes for commercial products of average strength and beverage type, have been intended for drinking with a meal.

Now let us suppose that the table is almost ready for clearing; the food has all gone and the general level of conversation has risen to a volume appropriate to the swankier night-spots of the Bahamas during the Duke And Duchess season. This is the time to bring out the rich, full-bodied dessert wines: zippier than anything so far considered.

To judge any wine by its alcohol content is as nonsensical as to assess the quality of a Yorkshire pudding by its weight, but these, if their strength is to lie within the desirable range of 15·6 to 17·0 per cent alcohol, will require far more sugar than any amount previously used and since experience has shown 32 oz (~~1·133 kilos~~) per gallon to be the maximum quantity upon which a yeast will produce around 10·5% alcohol in a short time and with ease, we needs must adapt our routines to compensate for its reluctance to work efficiently, without burping, on the additional ounces we now intend to thrust upon it.

Our aids to this are:

(a) the administration of sugar, reduced to the form of an Invert Syrup, by stages,

(b) the use of "classified" yeasts (as opposed to those of an all-purpose nature) and their activation by means of something universally known as a "starter bottle", and

(c) an appreciation (obtained by means of a hydrometer) of how much natural sugar our basic ingredients are themselves able to contribute to the Musts made from them.

The yeast/sugar relationship

Faced by more than the moderate amount of sugar for which it was biologically designed to cope, yeast becomes a choosey feeder. If we place ourselves, figuratively speaking, in its situation: seated at our imaginary table and served with every single item of an extensive menu on one swimming, brimming and totally revolting plate we can perhaps understand its reaction. Under such circumstances we should not, I think, get far beyond our napkin; yet if the same items, in exactly similar portions, are fed to us in a civilised manner, bit by bit and at discreet intervals, we can wolf the lot and still find the desire, when only the crumbs remain, to reach for the nuts or the lady of the house according to our inclinations.

Accept this comparison as a means of understanding the yeast/sugar relationship and you will appreciate the extent to which we can assist the fermentation process, and minimise the risk of its coming to a sudden halt, by adopting a "sugar-by-stages" technique.

Successive additions in the dry "straight from the packet" form are not, however, the answer since these (unless they can be very thoroughly incorporated by means of a good deal of relentless stirring) tend to lie around producing heavy layers of solid crystals or over-saturated solution that buy the yeast. Further, since it is far too easy to forget the increased bulk of the final product induced by each contribution, they tend to upset all calculations, causing us to run out of jar space with more sugar still needing to be added.

The avoidance of both these problems lies in the use of a heavy invert syrup that can be made up, bottled and labelled for use as required. Since, however, the qualification "Invert" may catch some readers unawares, it calls for an explanation.

Invert Sugar

To the layman, "sugar" means only the white granulated, cubed, castor, icing or slightly moist brown stuff by means of which he cushions the impact of other palate experiences and plays havoc with the calories. In point of fact, a remarkably wide range of substances come under the same heading and are, by the chemist, classified and subdivided into extensive lists of precise names with which, except for three, we have no concern.

"Sucrose" is sugar as we buy it. Not entirely unknown to yeasts in their natural surroundings (plums, for example, contain a high proportion of it and peaches depend upon it almost entirely for their sweetness) sucrose does, however, present certain problems so far as yeasts are concerned. Their appetites are for the sugars "fructose" and "glucose". These, closely related but left and right handed as it were, are both combinations of carbon, hydrogen and oxygen: combinations that inevitably come to grief when yeast cells are present.

What happens is this: one-third of the carbon and two-thirds of the oxygen break away, combine and escape as carbon dioxide gas. The remaining carbon and oxygen, plus the whole of the hydrogen, form a new complex group and become alcohol. Supplied only with packeted sugar, therefore, the yeasts of our choice have some initial disentangling to do. Putting their in-built chemistry to work, their first task must be to re-arrange the elements that compose the substance into two groups constituting fructose and glucose respectively, or to "invert" them.

The time taken for this, though it may be measured in hours rather than days, nevertheless applies a brake to the start of fermentation proper. It is, therefore, in our interest to speed things up as far as possible by doing a little sucrose-inverting on our own account, thus leaving the yeast free to concentrate on the more important matters in hand. Further, the resulting syrup enables us to make stage-by-stage sugar additions in an easily involved form and simplifies whatever calculations are required to ensure that, when all things are assembled down to the last ounce, the sum total of our product amounts exactly to the volume anticipated.

The process by which we induce the inversion of sucrose, by chemical rather than enzymic means, is easy to follow and will come as a natural routine to anyone who has followed the procedures so far reported upon. Nevertheless, here it is, set down in diagrammatic form, to avoid the possibility of anyone getting lost in the hit-or-miss. Each 20 fl oz (568 cc) of the resulting syrup provides 16 oz (453 gm) of truly inverted sugar, smaller additions of which can be made in accordance with Table F.

TO PREPARE INVERT SUGAR

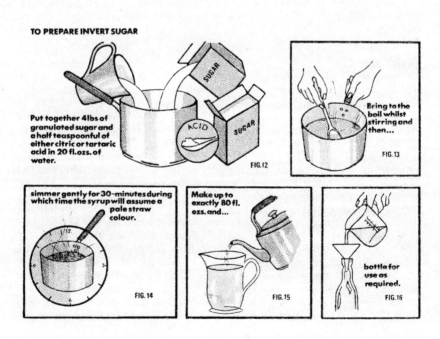

Put together 4 lbs of granulated sugar and a half teaspoonful of either citric or tartaric acid in 20 fl.ozs. of water.
FIG.12

Bring to the boil whilst stirring and then...
FIG.13

simmer gently for 30-minutes during which time the syrup will assume a pale straw colour.
FIG.14

Make up to exactly 80 fl. ozs. and...
FIG.15

bottle for use as required.
FIG.16

VOLUME OF SYRUP		WEIGHT OF INVERT SUGAR	
fl.ozs.	ccs.	ozs.	gms.
20·0	568	16	453
17·5	497	14	397
15·0	426	12	340
12·5	355	10	283
10·0	284	8	227
7·5	213	6	170
5·0	142	4	113
2·5	71	2	57
1·25	36	1	28

TABLE F

Classified yeasts

Over the first several hundred years of winemaking it was generally believed that good or evil spirits, rather than good or evil yeasts, hovered over every brew, dictating quality of output according to which was the stronger. Only gradually did folk latch on to the realisation that the influences controlling their pots had shape and form by means of which they might be identified and sorted. Even then, many more years were to pass before one particular species of yeast — Saccharomyces ellipsoideus — could be isolated, worked over, refined and cossetted for the benefit of amateur and commercial winemakers alike. The study of this (covering the flavour it is capable of injecting, the rate of fermentation it induces and its tolerance of alcohol strengths far in excess of any so far called for) has long been the purpose of researchers throughout the world.

To-day, in commercial laboratories, sealed phials lie resting in tiled cells, under lock and key. These contain pure cultures, rich in all the characteristics responsible for the famous names of wines with "Appelation of Origin", meticulously persuaded from superlative specimens collected from the finest grapes of the most renowned vineyards.

Subjected to treatment by special and very secret nutrient mediums, encouraged to develop by automatically assessed degrees of temperature and acidity, washed and eventually separated by centrifuge, the aristocratic descendants of these exemplary captives, finally persuaded into miniaturised test-tubes or sachets, merely await the right environment in order to achieve the purposes we have in mind for them. The names applied, however, are merely clues to their character. A yeast labelled "Champagne", for instance, will not necessarily produce a wine of champagne flavour. All that can be expected from it, with any degree of certainty, is a sediment of sandy nature; one that won't stick to the sides of a bottle and which may be shaken down on to the cork of its container if the latter is inverted as in commercial practice. Similarly, yeasts identified as "Port", "Malaga" or "Madeira" all have a tendency to render a wine extra flavoursome and tawny, whilst a "Burgundy" classification is a guarantee that the yeast so named will leave maximum colour in a wine intended to be richly-red.

Both the liquid and dried-granule forms of yeast have their supporting and critical factions. Having tried pretty well around the ring (for there are not many producers: the companies run to size and age, simplifying matters for the newcomer) we would say that both are equally effective. On the subject of wine *types*, however, we can be more specific; selecting six according to personal choice and listing some general observations as follows:

WINE YEASTS: A GUIDE TO THEIR CHOICE	TABLE G
TYPE	COMMENTS
BURGUNDY	Provides a strong fermentation and a firm sediment that is easy to handle and which leaves maximum colour and body in fruit wines. Particularly recommended for dry and medium-sweet wines based on bilberries, bullace, cherries, damsons, elderberries, plums and redcurrants, or for sweet wines based on blackberries or sloes.
COLD FERMENTATION ALL PURPOSE (Kaltgarhefe)	A specialist yeast, available under the brand name "Vierka", conforming to the run of all-purpose yeasts in general (insofar as it may be used in both red and white wines intended to be of a strength not exceeding 15·6% alcohol) but developed to provide good results at temperatures down to 42°Fa (6°Cent).

MADEIRA	Having a high alcohol potential (approximately 18% by volume) is best suited to full-bodied red wines of the dessert type which may, however, be rendered slightly tawny. Reacts well to a slight but deliberate oxidation and particularly recommended for use in wines based on mulberries, prunes or rosehips.
PORT	Variable as regards their alcohol potential but capable of injecting an extra richness of flavour into tawny dessert wines in which maximum "fruitiness" is required, yeasts of this type are particularly recommended for the fermentation of wines based on bilberries, blackcurrants, damsons, elderberries, mulberries, pears, plums, raspberries or sloes.
SAUTERNES	Imparts a slight but appropriate flavour to full-bodied sweet wines (white) within the range of 12%-15% alcohol by volume. Easily inhibited by sulphite additions (in the form of Campden Tablets) and thus ideal for the production of medium-sweet wines that may need to have their fermentation brought to a halt. Particularly recommended for use in wines based on apples, apricots, crab-apples, cranberries, currants, gooseberries, quinces, rhubarb, strawberries and white currants.
TOKAY	A high alcohol yeast pre-eminent for the production of quality dessert wines. It assists the development of bouquet and reacts well to slight temperature increases but gives a powdery deposit. Adequate racking is, thus, essential. Particularly recommended for the fermentation of wines based on bananas, dates, figs, mixed dried fruits, peaches, pineapples or raisins.

Although all types of yeast may be added directly to a prepared Must, delay is bound to follow if the amount is small in comparison with the volume of liquor to be treated. Following their admission the microscopic cells, in a dormant state as purchased, will, for some time, apparently do nothing.

The calm, as it happens, is misleading. Secretly and way beyond our range of vision, generation upon generation of them will be stirring to activity with a dedication of purpose that would do credit to a saint posing for stained glass. Each single fluid ounce of our prospective wine needs, however, to contain upwards of six-thousand-million healthy, rampaging cells before their show is open to the public. It pays us, therefore, to add a proportionately large amount of yeast to a few ounces only of some well aerated and growth encouraging medium in which it may develop away from all disturbing influences. Pampered thus, a vigorous and thriving colony will soon evolve and this, added to the bulk of our prospective wine, will ensure a sound fermentation within a comparatively short time.

Starter bottles

The preparation of these, depicted in the illustrations that follow, is simple and worthwhile, offering several advantages other than those concerned with the multiplication of the parent yeasts under ideal conditions. Their contents can be kept ready for use as required: be held in a quiescent state (at a temperature of 35°-40°Fa or 2°-4°Cent) or have their performance extended as necessary by the addition of a little extra sugar. It is also worth noting that only three-quarters or so of the activated solution need be added to a Must at any one time: thus the remaining quantity, topped up with freshly made medium, will produce further yeast growth and so remain capable of use ad infinitum or for as long, at least, as it remains free of infection.

THE PREPARATION OF A STARTER BOTTLE

(a) Fig. 17 / Fig. 18 (b) Fig. 19
To the juice of a large orange add an equal quantity of water and a teaspoonful of sugar. — Bring to the boil for one minute.

(c) Fig. 20 (d) Fig. 21 (e) Fig. 22
Transfer to sterilised bottle as soon as possible, then cool quickly under cold tap. — When cold introduce yeast and shake bottle well (uncorked) to aerate. — Plug the neck with cotton wool and leave in a warm atmosphere (e.g. an airing cupboard).

Sugar assessment

Whatever the nature of the basic winemaking ingredients we intend to use, be they fresh fruits, bottled juices, syrups or concentrates, all will have some sugar of their own to contribute.

So far (by keeping our own subscriptions of household granulated to modest levels) we have been able to ignore the fact. From this point on, however, we shall be aiming for alcohol strengths bordering on the limits of yeast tolerance, and if we are to avoid the risk of producing grossly over-sweet wines we need to have some means of calculating the amount of sugar supplied by the ingredients themselves.

So far as fresh fruits are concerned, a fair estimation may be obtained by reference to the Table that follows in which the commonest of fruits, assumed to be of average ripeness, are listed alongside the approximate weight of their sugar content.

TABLE H

FRUIT	AVAILABLE QUANTITY OF NATURAL SUGAR PER LB OF PICKED WEIGHT	
	Oz	Gm
Apples	1·60	45
Apricots	·96	27
Bananas	2·88	82
Bilberries	1·60	45
Blackberries	·96	27
Blackcurrants	1·12	32
Cherries	1·60	45
Dried Bananas	9·50	269
Elderberries	1·28	36
Figs	1·92	55
Gooseberries	·96	27
Loganberries	·96	27
Mulberries	1·28	36
Peaches	1·44	41
Pears	1·60	45
Plums	1·60	45
Quince	·80	23
Raisins	9·50	269
Raspberries	·96	27
Redcurrants	·80	23
Sloes	1·28	36
Strawberries	·96	27
Sultanas	9·50	269

For the purpose of illustrating the Table in use, let us suppose that we intend to follow a one-gallon recipe that calls for the addition of 2 lb (907 gm) of elderberries and an equal quantity of blackberries, a total of 3 lb (1·360 kilos) of sugar being required to give us a medium-sweet wine of 14% alcohol. Then our elderberries will supply 2 × 1·28 ounces of sugar (2·56 oz or 72 gm) and our blackberries 2 × ·96 (1·92 oz or 54 gm) making a total of almost 4½ ounces: more than enough to send our wine "over the top" unless we take account of it by reducing our input of household granulated by a similar amount to compensate.

Although serving to underline the importance of ascertaining how much sugar any type of basic ingredient supplies, and the necessity of making allowance for it, such calculations as those referred to can only prove adequate in the case of wines made by those who may not be too fussy and cannot, of course, serve any purpose at all as regards wines made from commercially available syrups, concentrates and such. These demand attentions of a different and more precise nature. If, therefore, you would prefer (for the moment, at least) to ignore the issues they involve, skip right along to the recipes that follow in which the initial sugar content of the ingredients recommended has been pre-assessed. If, on the other hand, you would really like to get to grips with the many-balled juggling trick that winemaking is, turn a deaf ear to those folk who rush to tell you that a hydrometer is a non-essential.

The Winemaker's Hydrometer

Simply stated, this is a sealed glass tube (containing three scales: one marked off in what common practice has elected shall be called "degrees of gravity" and the others headed "sugar content" and "potential alcohol" respectively) so weighted that it floats in water to a depth at which the surface cuts the gravity scale at a point marked "00": a symbol representing 1,000 since it has been universally agreed that this figure should be accepted as the "gravity" of water.

Needless to say, this is an arbitrary arrangement but one that works very well for our convenience since any substance (sugar, for example) dissolved in water will have the effect of increasing the latter's gravity, causing the hydrometer to ride higher and higher in the solution according to the weight of soluble matter involved. Thus, by noting the number of degrees of gravity registered by any juice or liquor and subtracting that basic figure of 1,000, we may accurately assess the amount of soluble matter contained in it, and though this will not all be sugar far less confusion will arise if we assume that it is.

As a preliminary to the complete understanding of the principle involved: float your hydrometer in water (preferably in a glass test-jar of a depth and width suited to the proportions of the instrument it partners but small enough to be comfortably held with the surface of its contents at eye level as in Fig. 23), impart a spin to its long stem (for the purpose of clearing any air bubbles that might adhere to it) and note the scale reading from fractionally below surface level (see Fig. 24-A).

Now dissolve two or three teaspoonfuls of sugar in the water and repeat the experiment. On this occasion the hydrometer will be found to float at a higher level, more of its stem protruding from the surface of the solution which, consequently, cuts the scale at a higher reading (Fig. 24-B).

By counting the extra number of degrees registered (ten in the case of our illustrated example) we ascertain the "gravity" of the syrup under test (which may now be said to have a gravity of ten) and this way of expressing the weight of our sugar solution (specifically compared with the weight of an equal volume of water) can then be translated into practical terms, either by reference to the "sugar content" and "potential alcohol" scales which the hydrometer itself incorporates or, if one needs to be more precise, the following Table I.

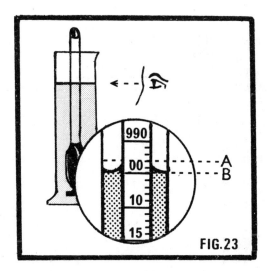

Take all hydrometer readings with the surface of the liquid slightly above eye-level. This prevents the eye being misled as shown here where B is the correct reading.

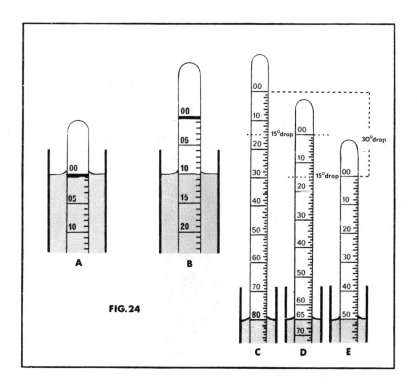

TABLE I		POTENTIAL STRENGTH OF FINISHED WINE		SURFACE READINGS
SUGAR CONTENT: per gallon		**% Alc. by volume if fermented to dry**		
Ozs.	Gms.			
			980	
			990	
			00	← Water
2	57	0.9 →	10	
4	113	1.6 →	15	
7	198	2.3 →	20	
9	255	3.0 →	25	
12	340	3.7 →	30	
15	425	4.4 →	35	
17	482	5.1 →	40	
19	539	5.8 →	45	
21	595	6.5 →	50	
23	652	7.2 →	55	
25	709	7.8 →	60	
27	765	8.6 →	65	
29	822	9.2 →	70	
31	879	9.9 →	75	
33	936	10.6 →	80	← Sugar solution (33oz. sugar/gal)
36	1021	11.3 →	85	
38	1077	12.0 →	90	
40	1134	12.7 →	95	
42	1191	13.4 →	100	← Sugar solution (42oz. sugar/gal)
44	1247	14.1 →	105	
46	1304	14.9 →	110	
48	1361	15.6 →	115	← Sugar solution (48oz. sugar/gal)
50	1417	16.3 →	120	
52	1474	17.0 →	125	← Sugar solution (52oz. sugar/gal)
54	1531	17.7 →	130	
56	1588	18.4 →	135	
			140	

Readings beyond this point indicate amounts of sugar exceeding yeast tolerance.

By tracing a finger across the columns of the Table we find that a *gallon* of thin syrup identical to our imaginary test sample would contain 2 oz (57 gm) of sugar and yield 0·9% alcohol if fermented to dryness. If, on the other hand, only half-a-gallon were available (but intended for further dilution to a one-gallon quantity) the gravity reading (and, in consequence, the amount of sugar and percentage of alcohol it promises) would need to be halved.

For the purpose of further clarifying this point, and illustrative of the hydrometer's use in connection with a variety of different ingredients, here are two examples:–

EXAMPLE 1

A recipe for a one-gallon quantity of wine intended to be of 15·6% alcohol (the result of fermenting a total of 3 lb — 1·361 kilos — of sugar to dryness) calls for the inclusion of 40 fl oz — 1·136 litres — of canned orange juice. Question: how much sugar will the orange juice itself provide?

In this case our first task must be to dilute the 40 fl oz of orange juice to exactly half-a-gallon.

A sample quantity of this dilution, transferred to a test jar, provides a hydrometer reading of, perhaps, 60-degrees indicating the presence of 25 oz (709 gm) of sugar *per gallon*. Since, however, we only have half that quantity we must halve the gravity reading in order to compensate and, subsequently transferring our attention to the "30-degree" figure of the Table, we learn that by using the whole half-gallon of diluted juice we shall gain the benefit of 12 oz (340 gm) of sugar. It is, then, easy to assess that only 2lb 4 oz (1·021 kilos) of supplementary household granulated will be required to achieve the strength intended.

EXAMPLE 2

A one-gallon recipe for a port-type wine of 17% alcohol (the result of fermenting 3 lb 4 oz — 1·474 kilos — of sugar to dryness) calls for the inclusion of 2 lb (907 gm) of bilberries, 1 lb (453 gm) of elderberries, 12 oz (340 gm) of dried apricots and 5 fl oz (142 cc) of red grape concentrate. Question: how much sugar will these combined ingredients provide?

Adopting the juice extraction technique now familiar to us, assemble the fruits in a plastic pail, pour on 4-pints (2·273 litres) of boiling water and, when this has cooled sufficiently, mash them all together between the fingers before adding the usual sulphite and enzyme preparations (i.e. Campden tablet, anti-pectin and Rohament P).

Leave in a warm atmosphere for 24-hours before straining off the juice, adding the grape concentrate and making up to exactly half-a-gallon quantity. From this point on the taking of a test-jar sample, the halving of the gravity reading a hydrometer provides and the assessment of supplementary sugar required is conducted as in the previous example.

Our understanding of these matters and our application of them to the job in hand is but a simple step, made easier by the fact that our particular interest lies in the production of fast-fermenting wines within the range of 10·6% alcohol (the strength of a good red or white burgundy) and 17% alcohol, at which point the zippier vermouths demand booster-doses of grape brandy: a situation that enables us to establish the following working routine:

For all wines of 10·6% alcohol intended to be "dry"

Total sugar content per British gallon (4·546 litres)		PROCEDURE
Oz	Gm	
33	936	Assemble all sugar together from the outset and ferment to dryness.

For all wines of 13·4% alcohol intended to be of medium sweetness

Total sugar content per British gallon (4·546 litres)		PROCEDURE
Oz	kilos	
42	1·191	Introduce sugar in two stages: an initial complement of 33 oz and a further addition of 9 oz (255 gm) in syrup form following the first seven days of active ferment.

For all wines of 15·6% alcohol intended to be "sweet"

Total sugar content per British gallon (4·546 litres)		PROCEDURE
Oz	kilos	
48	1·361	Introduce sugar in three stages: the first two as above and the third (6 oz or 170 gm in syrup form) following the first fourteen days of active ferment.

For aperitifs and port-type dessert wines of 17·0% alcohol

Total sugar content per British gallon (4·546 litres)		PROCEDURE
Oz	kilos	
52	1·474	Introduce sugar in four stages: the first three as above and the final addition of 4 oz (113 gm) in syrup form following the first nineteen days of active ferment.

In all cases a hydrometer reading of the fermenting wine can be useful as a means of ascertaining its progress towards completion (and who, having started to produce the stuff, would be content to wait for Bacchus on the beach when we can, as it were, wade to meet him!)? Let us suppose that, having put a dry table wine together and immediately prior to the addition of any yeast, we take a test sample of it and note a gravity reading of 80-degrees (Fig. 24-C). Successive tests, made during the course of fermentation, will show the hydrometer to be gradually sinking, degree by degree, under the influence of the alcohol (lighter than water) being developed around it. Following the first day or so of our air-lock's energetic activity we may, conceivably, find gravity reduced to 65-degrees (Fig. 24-D): a drop of fifteen degrees which we see, by further reference to Table I, indicates the presence of 1·6% alcohol.

By the time a further test is made the gravity might be down to 50-degrees: a total drop of thirty, confirming the development of 3·7% alcohol (Fig. 24-E).

And so on, down to complete dryness. It is, however, necessary to bear in mind the fact that all hydrometers are graduated by their manufacturers to be accurate at one pre-determined temperature, noted on the scale itself and usually 60°Fa (15°Cent). We, on the other hand, will be applying our periodic tests to samples having temperatures in the range of 70°-77°Fa (21°-25°Cent). If, therefore, our readings are to be as accurate as possible we need to make allowances, by addition or subtraction, in accordance with the temperature/gravity correction Table J that follows.

TABLE J—Gravity corrections and temperatures relevant to express winemaking

		TEMPERATURE ° FAHRENHEIT	TEMPERATURE ° CENTIGRADE	GRAVITY CORRECTION	TABLE J GRAVITY CORRECTIONS AND TEMPERATURES RELEVANT TO EXPRESS WINEMAKING
Lowest theoretical fermentation temp.	→	4 6	7·8		
Serve white/rose wines	→ {	4 8	8·9		
		5 0	10·0	−0·6	
		5 2	11·0	−0·5	
		5 4	12·2	−0·4	
Mature and store wines within temperatures	→ {	5 6	13·3	−0·2	
		5 8	14·4	−0·1	
		6 0	15·5	CORRECT	
Serve red wines	→ {	6 2	16·7	+0·2	
		6 4	17·8	+0·4	
		6 6	18·9	+0·6	
		6 8	20·0	+0·8	
Recommended ferment- ation temperatures	→ {	7 0	21·1	+1·1	
		7 2	22·2	+1·3	
		7 4	23·3	+1·6	
		7 6	24·3	+1·8	
		7 8	25·6	+2·1	
Not to be exceeded	→	8 0	26·7	+2·4	

Here, now, are some recipes for medium-sweet or sweet wines with which to accompany the crisps and nuts, turn night into an anachronism or break your lease.

Alcohol strengths of between 13·4% and 17·0% are appropriate and fermentations are best brought to a final halt (by the addition of potassium sorbate and a couple of Campden tablets) when final sugar additions are reduced to gravity readings between 10 and 20 degrees.

APPLE AND PEACH

Ingredients for 1-gallon
        9 fl oz (256 cc) apple concentrate,
        8 fl oz (227 cc) white grape concentrate,
        1 × 30 oz (850 gm) can of peaches,
        16 oz (453 gm) granulated sugar,
        20 fl oz (568 cc) Invert sugar syrup,
        1 teaspoon (5 gm) tartaric acid,
        ½ teaspoon (2·5 gm) Rohament P,
        1 teaspoon (5 gm) anti-pectin enzyme,
        7 fl oz (86 cc) Wyoming Bentonite suspension,
        1 tablespoon (15 cc) potassium sorbate solution,
        3 Campden tablets,
        Sauternes wine yeast,
        Nutrient salts.

Method
Day 1: Prepare the yeast in the form of a Starter Bottle (see page 54), plugging the neck of the container with a twist of cottonwool and leaving it in a warm atmosphere for fermentation to commence.

Day 2: Mash the peaches and combine them, plus their surrounding syrup, with the concentrates in a plastic pail or other suitable wide-mouthed vessel. Pour on 2½-pints (1·420 litres) of lukewarm water and stir in one crushed Campden tablet, the anti-pectin and Rohament P before covering with a clean towel and leaving for 24-hours in a warm atmosphere.

Day 3: Strain off the juice and adjust its volume to exactly half-a-gallon (2·273 litres). It is at this point those desiring to do so may take their initial gravity reading, remembering to *halve* the figure recorded and adjusting subsequent sugar additions according to their personal inclinations. Those of a less enquiring nature should, however, proceed by dissolving the acid, granulated sugar and nutrient salts in 1½-pints (852 cc) of lukewarm water, combining the resultant solution with the juice in a fermentation jar, adding 3½ fl oz (43 cc) of Wyoming Bentonite suspension and swirling everything into complete involvement. The activation of the brew (by means of the Starter Bottle) and the capping of the jar with an air-lock then follows.

Left in an atmosphere of 75°Fa (24°Cent) the main bulk of Must should be in full ferment within a matter of hours and a gentle rock, imparted each day, will aid its progress towards the point when, on Day 11, further sugar may be added.

Day 11: Add the invert syrup, shaking this well into the developing wine, and leave the fermentation to proceed until it slows to a very appreciable extent or, if you do not consider the use of a hydrometer too complicated, a test sample reveals that a gravity between 10 and 15 degrees has been achieved. Then proceed exactly as from Stage 7 of the original Vin Blanc Express No. 1 recipe.

APPLE AND RAISIN

This is a sweet and full-bodied dessert wine in which alcohol strength and flavour are well represented.

Ingredients for 1-gallon
      20 fl oz (568 cc) apple concentrate,
      16 oz (453 gm) raisins,
      10 oz (283gm) granulated sugar,
      27 fl oz (767 cc) Invert sugar syrup,
      ½ teaspoon (2·5 gm) Rohament P,
      1 teaspoon (5 gm) anti-pectin enzyme,
      7 fl oz (86 cc) Wyoming Bentonite suspension,
      1 tablespoon (15 cc) potassium sorbate solution,
      3 Campden tablets,
      Burgundy wine yeast,
      Nutrient salts.

Method
Day 1: Prepare a Burgundy yeast starter in the manner previously described.
Day 2: Wash and chop the raisins, combine them with the apple concentrate and pour on 2½-pints (1·420 litres) of boiling water. Leave until only lukewarm, then stir in one crushed Campden tablet, the anti-pectin and Rohament P before covering with a clean towel and leaving in a warm atmosphere for 24-hours.
Day 3: Adjust the volume of strained juice to exactly half-a-gallon. Dissolve the granulated sugar and nutrient salts in 1-pint (568 cc) of lukewarm water and combine both liquors (by vigorous shaking) in the fermentation vessel before swirling in 3½ fl oz of Wyoming Bentonite suspension and activating by the addition of the starter bottle contents which should, by now, be in full ferment.

Apply air-lock and leave to ferment in an atmosphere adjusted to 75°Fa (24°Cent).

The subsequent addition of invert sugar syrup (shaken into complete involvement) should be made in three stages as follows:-

14 fl oz (398 cc) following the first seven days of active ferment, 9 fl oz (256 cc) following the first fourteen days of active ferment and, finally, 4 fl oz (114 cc) following the first nineteen days of active ferment. From this point, fermentation should be allowed to proceed, under lock, until it slows to a very appreciable extent or a hydrometer test provides a gravity reading in the region of 20-degrees. Then proceed as from Stage 7 of the original Vin Blanc Express No. 1 recipe.

BILBERRY AND BANANA

You will be less than human if you do not feel inclined to drink this full-bodied red dessert wine immediately. Do, however, try to put at least two bottles down to mature!

Ingredients for 1-gallon
        32 oz (907 gm) bilberries,
        4 oz (113 gm) dried bananas,
        8 oz (226 gm) sultanas,
        16 oz (453 gm) granulated sugar,
        40 fl oz (1·137 litres) Invert sugar syrup,
        1 teaspoon (5 gm) citric acid,
        ½ teaspoon (2·5 gm) Rohament P,
        1 teaspoon (5 gm) anti-pectin enzyme,
        7 fl oz (86 cc) Wyoming Bentonite suspension,
        1 tablespoon (15 cc) potassium sorbate solution,
        3 Campden tablets,
        Madiera wine yeast,
        Nutrient salts.

Method
Day 1: Prepare yeast starter bottle.
Day 2: Simmer the bilberries and bananas together in 4-pints (2·273 litres) of water for ten minutes. At the conclusion of this time pour the contents of the saucepan, still hot, over the minced sultanas and, when only lukewarm, stir in one crushed Campden tablet, the anti-pectin enzyme and Rohament P before covering with a clean towel and leaving in a warm atmosphere for 24-hours.
Day 3: Strain the juice free of any solid material and, having made its volume up to half-a-gallon, dissolve in it the granulated sugar, acid and nutrient salts before transferring it to the fermenting vessel. The addition of 3½ fl oz (43 cc) of Wyoming Bentonite suspension and the activated yeast starter then follows.

Left to ferment in a 75°Fa (24°Cent) temperature for seven days, the developing wine is ready to receive its first booster dose of 20 fl oz (568 cc) of invert sugar syrup. This should be well swirled into complete involvement and fermentation allowed to continue for a further week following which a second dose (15 fl oz or 426 cc) may be applied. The final addition of 5 fl oz (142 cc) made five days later is then allowed to ferment to a finish or to a gravity reading of 8-degrees when the application of further Wyoming Bentonite suspension, Campden tablets and potassium sorbate solution follows in accordance with the routines previously detailed.

BILBERRY, ELDERBERRY AND APRICOT

This is a rich and full-bodied dessert wine of the Port type, formulated to mature quickly.

Ingredients for 1-gallon
32 oz (907 gm) bilberries,
16 oz (453 gm) elderberries,
12 oz (340 gm) dried apricots,
5 fl oz (142 cc) red grape concentrate,
24 oz (680 gm) granulated sugar,
30 fl oz (852 cc) Invert sugar syrup,
½ teaspoon (2·5 gm) Rohament P,
1 teaspoon (5 gm) anti-pectin enzyme,
7 fl oz (86 cc) Wyoming Bentonite suspension,
1 tablespoon (15 cc) potassium sorbate solution,
3 Campden tablets,
Port wine yeast,
Nutrient salts.

Method
Day 1: Prepare yeast starter bottle.
Day 2: Assemble the fruits in a large saucepan, pour on 3-pints (1·705 litres) of water and bring to a gentle simmer for ten minutes; then allow to cool and, when only lukewarm, stir in one crushed Campden tablet, the anti-pectin enzyme and Rohament P before covering with a clean towel and leaving in a warm atmosphere for 24-hours.
Day 3: Strain off the juice, add the red grape concentrate and make up to a half-gallon quantity.

Dissolve the granulated sugar and nutrient salts in 1½-pints (852 cc) of lukewarm water and combine both liquors in the fermentation vessel before swirling in 3½ fl oz (43 cc) of Wyoming Bentonite suspension followed by the contents of the starter bottle.

Apply air-lock and leave to ferment (in a temperature of 75°Fa or 24°Cent) for one week; then involve 20 fl oz (568 cc) of invert sugar syrup. One week later add a further 6 fl oz (170 cc) of the syrup and make the final addition of 4 fl oz (114 cc) following the first nineteen days of activity through the lock.

The wine should subsequently be allowed to ferment to a finish, the addition of further Wyoming Bentonite suspension, potassium sorbate solution and so on being carried out as detailed in the original recipe for Vin Blanc Express No. 1.

BLACKCURRANT SYRUP AND DRIED BANANA

This, somewhat surprisingly, is not a red wine; nor does it taste of either of the main ingredients, falling rather into the category of a dry sherry-type aperitif.

Ingredients for 1-gallon
12 fl oz (340 cc) "Ribena" blackcurrant syrup,
6 oz (170 gm) dried bananas,
16 oz (453 gm) granulated sugar,
30 fl oz (852 cc) Invert sugar syrup,
½-teaspoon (2·5 gm) Rohament P,
1 teaspoon (5 gm) anti-pectin enzyme,
7 fl oz (86 cc) Wyoming Bentonite suspension,
1 tablespoon (15 cc) potassium sorbate solution,
3 Campden tablets,
Burgundy wine yeast,
Nutrient salts.

Method
Day 1: Prepare starter bottle.
Day 2: Simmer the bananas in 2-pints (1·137 litres) of water for ten minutes, then allow to cool and, when only lukewarm, stir in one crushed Campden tablet, the anti-pectin enzyme and Rohament P. Cover with a clean towel and leave in a warm atmosphere for 24-hours.
Day 3: Strain off the juice, mix with the blackcurrant syrup and adjust to half-gallon volume.

Dissolve the granulated sugar and nutrient salts in 1-pint (568 cc) of lukewarm water and combine both liquors in a fermentation jar before involving 3½ fl oz (43 cc) of Wyoming Bentonite suspension and the prepared yeast starter.

Leave to ferment under lock, adding invert sugar syrup stage by stage as in the previous recipe, and eventually finish off by adding further Wyoming Bentonite suspension, potassium sorbate solution and Campden tablets as detailed in the original Vin Blanc Express No. 1 recipe.

CHAPTER TEN

Hail and Inhale

Once you have sipped enough wines to form your own judgements you may decide that they are at their best when served from a bucket and dipper, swigged from the bottle, watered with ice-cubes or taken by injection. The "rules", after all, are nothing but majority opinion. There are, however, a few suggestions we can offer to make the downing of your pick-ups even downier.

At the time of their final clearance (whether or not this has needed to be helped on its way by the addition of a fining agent) they will, of course, be very young and possibly a little sharp. This rawness will quickly disappear over the course of a few weeks but in the event of some spontaneous challenge a dessertspoon (10 cc) or so of glycerine, slipped into each gallon, will smooth things out quite considerably.

Given time in which to mature naturally, wines achieve their best when stored in bulk, preferably at a temperature between 57°–60°Fa (14°–16°Cent) 'though this may be slightly exceeded without cause for undue alarm. Nor need one feel concerned over the appearance of any sandy, insoluble, crystals that may materialise at the bottom of the jar. This is a to-be-expected and, indeed, welcomed development indicative of the fact that slight excesses (principally of an acidic nature) are precipitating, leading to an increased quality of flavour.

In all cases, wines are best bottled at the temperature intended for their storage and should be so adjusted as to leave a half-inch space between their surface and the underside of the cork that seals them. Only true wine bottles (greenish glass for the reds and rosés; clear for the white or golden) fitted with new corks should be used since nothing degrades a product more, in the eyes of one's guests, than a container inappropriate to it. There are, also, sound practical reasons for such fastidiousness. The rim of the punt serves to grip any minor sedimentation, the colour of the glass protects red and rosé wines from undue exposure to light, and the use of old corks is a false economy anyway since these can be the source of contaminations by which even the strongest wines, braced with alcohol as they are, may be affected.

New corks, available in a variety of standard types (some more suited to a simple push-and-twist technique than others which are best applied by means of a corking tool), should always be softened before use if they are to give the best possible service. Left to soak overnight in a little water or sulphite solution to which a teaspoon or so of glycerine has been added they swell slightly and become more manageable, adjusting themselves exactly to the dimensions of the bottle neck into which they are forced. Alternatively, they may be floated in a shallow depth of water brought to boiling and used immediately. In this case, however, care must be taken to ensure that the corks are not themselves boiled, otherwise they lose much of their nature and disintegrate when opening time comes round.

The "pop" of a healthy cork is encouraging. Even the tone-deaf smile and nod in anticipatory pleasure at the sound. It is invariably associated with the pleasant beginnings of things, never the end, and it signifies that the controlled amount of air originally below the cork has been absorbed by the wine, leading to the development of maturity and bouquet. Referring to the white and rosé table wines mentioned, this may follow within a matter of days, the red wines benefiting from being left undisturbed for several weeks longer. All, however, will remain sound for at least two years in bottle 'though no further improvement in quality can be expected after six months. The stronger dessert and aperitif types, on the other hand, will continue to improve significantly for three years but should be drunk and enjoyed within five.

Now let us take a broad view on entertaining. You can curl up with a good bottle by yourself without any undue planning. As a host or hostess you have a moral obligation to serve your wines in the manner most calculated to suit your guests (not to be confused with the spongers who deserve only the worst you have short of poison. If they like your stuff too much, they might come back too often!). So display your bottles proudly, with nary a clinker amongst them, and let them stand for 24-hours at room temperature. Then, if you wish to chill them (and ideally the serving temperature for white and rosé wines is 46°-50°Fa or 8°-10°Cent) put them in a refrigerator for an hour or so, or set the bottles in a bucket of ice for twenty or thirty minutes.

Long matured red wines are best decanted a few hours before being served. If the bottle has been stored in the generally approved fashion (lying down, so that the bubble of air within it is clear of the cork) it should be stood upright and left overnight so that any sediment may settle to the bottom. Then the outside of the neck is wiped, the cork extracted and the inside of the neck cleaned; all these tasks being conducted with the utmost care to ensure that the bottle is never jarred or knocked.

Finally the old wine is poured, gently and steadily, into the new vessel until the first traces of sediment appear in its stream which should be continuously observed by means of a candle light or bare opal bulb behind it. The small quantity of unclear wine that remains may then be filtered through a piece of dry but well rinsed muslin or a filter paper.

Most table wines, and certainly the red ones, benefit from being aired for an hour or two before being served. If, however, a fresh bottle is called for during the course of a meal, rub the rim of its neck with a small piece of waxed paper. This prevents dripping.

Spillage may be further avoided if the bottle is given a twist to the right or left as you complete pouring.

Preferred glasses for all but sparkling wines are tulip-shaped, un-ornamented, colourless and stemmed: an arrangement that serves three major purposes, ensuring that the aromas of their contents are not dissipated as they leave the surface, enabling the colour and clarity of the wine to be appreciated without distraction, and providing for chilled wines to be held without risk of the hand imparting its warmth. It is, however, desirable that the walls of the bowl should be as thin as possible so that, in the case of red wines, a degree of handwarmth can be deliberately applied to unleash those vestiges of bouquet that might otherwise be lost.

A word of warning before we go into further detail:

Refuse to be intimidated by any mumbo-jumbo regarding intricate serving rituals and ignore those anxious to offer high-faluting do's and don't's respecting the ways in which to handle the precious stuff the vintners sell. It can be argued, quite reasonably, that any good wine "goes" with practically any good dish. In any case, the majority of these gratuitous advices, based on an experience of commercial wines as distinct from those we make ourselves, are so much excess bag and baggage. Since, however, we needs must know the rules before we break them, here are some specific guidelines, concerning food and laid down by the experts, to accept or ignore according to your fancy:

Whilst sherry-type wines can be drunk with almost anything, red wines, generally speaking, do not go well with fish or egg dishes and certainly not with hors d'oeuvre, oysters, prawn-cocktails, soup, chicken or light meats of any sort. For these a dry white wine makes an appropriate accompaniment, the reds being reserved for serving with game, roasts and any red meats you may care to name.

Rosé wines partner spicy dishes and all light meats in a fitting manner, whilst sweet white wines are at their best with melon, strawberries, compote of fresh fruits or, indeed, any form of sweet or dessert. Either red or white wines will serve to complement the pleasures of the cheese board and full-bodied richly red wines excellently follow coffee and the passing of the nuts.

To be even more specific: wines largely based on apples make an excellent pre-luncheon drink and have the advantage of blending well with both fish and meat dishes on those less-than-formal occasions during which only one wine is considered necessary. Bilberry wines, fermented to dryness, add something special to meat dishes (particularly steaks, grilled lamb cutlets and roasts) whilst elderberry wines, treated the same way, blend well with meats but also possess the ability to slip naturally, and beneficently, into vegetarian menus.

Wines based on gooseberries and made medium-sweet are an approved accompaniment for all fish courses of pronounced flavour (e.g. prawn-cocktail, Sole Normande or grilled plaice) whilst, if fermented to dryness, they enter into a perfect marriage with several cheeses, the French "Brie" cheese in particular.

One final point . . .

The stomach best equipped to handle itself in a respectable manner under all circumstances is the one kept fully employed. Water-biscuits or cream-crackers topped with cubes of cheese, salted nuts and potato crisps may suffice to steer a group of well mannered guests through a single glass of something fairly light and dry. If, however, you open your cellar to them there will come a time when the investigating brethren, convinced that your home made and express product holds greater possibilities than their first glass had room for, will start ignoring the tit-bits and looking around for solids: substantial cold cuts or multi-storied open sandwiches that may be relied upon to fight back. Serve them nursery-sized scrambled-egg soldiers at this point and they will, quite rightly, hate you for ever.

Index

71

- acidity of 5
- sugar content 55
Rhubarb: acidity of 5
Ribena syrup 36
Rohament P 40, 41, 46
- dosage 41
- application 41
- terminating effect of 47
Roseberry puree 32
Rosehips: acidity of 5
Rowanberries 27
- acidity of 5

S

Saccharoyces ellipsoideus 51
Sediment traps 13
- method of use 18
- types of 16, 17
Silicic acis 26
Siphoning 16, 18
Sloes: acidity of 5
- sugar content 55
Sodium metabisulphate 19, 20, 29
- stock solution 26, 29
- pyrosulphite 23
Spanish Clay 23
Stabilising compound 6, 25
Starter bottles 48
- versatilety of 54
- preparation 54
Strawberries 26
- acidity of 5
- sugar content 55
Sucrose 49
Sugar 13, 48, 49
- addition of 49,50
- alcohol from 8, 48
- assessment of 54, 58, 59
- inversion of 48, 49, 50, 51
- yeast relationship 49
Sulphite compounds 23, 26
- solution 14, 20, 68
Sulphur dioxide 19
Sultanas: acidity of 5
- sugar content 55

T

Tangerines: acidity of 5
Tannin 6, 28, 29, 44, 46
Tartar 26
Tartaric acid 5, 20, 23, 27
Temperature 7, 8, 61, 67, 68
- adjustment of 13, 61

Thiamine 24
Tronozymol 24, 29

V

Vigneron 21, 22
Vinamat 21, 22, 26
Vitamin B1 24

W

Whitecurrants: acidity of 5
Wine bottles 67
Wine decanting 68, 69
- seving 68, 69
- storage 68
Wyoming Bentonite 6, 23, 26
- preparation of 24
- rate of use 24

Y

Yeasts 6, 13, 23, 24, 25, 48, 51
-alcohol tolerance of 13, 54
- preparation of 25
- sugar relationship 49
- types 52, 53
- wild 19
Yellow prussiate of potash 26

Z

Zinc sulphate 26